SELECTIONS FROM
MORNING AND

Evening

CHARLES H. SPURGEON

BARBOUR
PUBLISHING, INC.
Uhrichsville, Ohio

© 2001 by Barbour Publishing, Inc.

ISBN 1-58660-036-2

Unless otherwise noted, all Scripture quotations are taken from the King James Version of the Bible.

Published by Barbour Publishing, Inc., P.O. Box 719, Uhrichsville, Ohio 44683 http://www.barbourbooks.com

 Member of the
Evangelical Christian
Publishers Association

Printed in the United States of America.

SELECTIONS FROM
MORNING AND

INTRODUCTION

The son and grandson of Christian ministers, Charles Haddon Spurgeon gave this high calling a new meaning. At the age of sixteen, Spurgeon accepted Christ as his Savior and soon afterward began sharing the gospel with others.

Shortly after his conversion, Spurgeon began his preaching ministry in Teversham, England, and the next year accepted a pastorate at the Baptist Chapel at Waterbeach. The church grew rapidly, and Spurgeon was called to London's New Park Street Baptist Church. By the age of twenty-one, he was London's most popular preacher.

The popularity of Spurgeon led to the publication of more than five dozen volumes of his sermons. He also published a number of other religious books including his well-loved devotional, *Morning and Evening*.

Over the years, *Morning and Evening* has brought much encouragement to its many readers. This abridged version, *Selections from Morning and Evening*, focuses primarily on those passages that speak of the love of God. It is our hope that through reading these segments you will gain a fuller understanding of what it means to be loved by God and to love with a Christ-like love.

Casting all your care upon him; for he careth for you.
1 Peter 5:7

It is a happy way of soothing sorrow when we can feel—
"He careth for me." Christian! do not dishonor religion by
always wearing a brow of care; come, cast your burden upon
your Lord. You are staggering beneath a weight which your
Father would not feel. What seems to you a crushing burden,
would be to Him but as the small dust of the balance. Nothing
is so sweet as to:

Lie passive in God's hands,
And know no will but His.

O child of suffering, be thou patient; God has not passed
thee over in His providence. He who is the feeder of sparrows,
will also furnish you with what you need. Sit not down in
despair; hope on, hope ever. Take up the arms of faith against
a sea of trouble, and your opposition shall yet end your dis-
tresses. There is One who careth for you. His eye is fixed on
you, His heart beats with pity for your woe, and His hand
omnipotent shall yet bring you the needed help. The darkest
cloud shall scatter itself in showers of mercy. The blackest
gloom shall give place to the morning. He, if thou art one of
His family, will bind up thy wounds, and heal thy broken heart.
Doubt not His grace because of thy tribulation, but believe that
He loveth thee as much in seasons of trouble as in times of
happiness. What a serene and quiet life might you lead if you
would leave providing to the God of providence! With a little
oil in the cruse, and a handful of meal in the barrel, Elijah out-
lived the famine, and you will do the same. If God cares for
you, why need you care, too? Can you trust Him for your soul,
and not for your body? He has never refused to bear your burdens, He has never fainted under their weight. Come, then,
soul! have done with fretful care, and leave all thy concerns in
the hand of a gracious God.

"Now the hand of the LORD was upon me in the evening.
EZEKIEL 33:22

In the way of judgment this may be the case, and, if so, be it mine to consider the reason of such a visitation and bear the rod and Him that hath appointed it. I am not the only one who is chastened in the night season; let me cheerfully submit to the affliction and carefully endeavor to be profited thereby. But the hand of the Lord may also be felt in another manner, strengthening the soul and lifting the spirit upward towards eternal things. O that I may in this sense feel the Lord dealing with me! A sense of the divine presence and indwelling bears the soul towards heaven as upon the wings of eagles. At such times we are full to the brim with spiritual joy, and forget the cares and sorrows of earth; the invisible is near, and the visible loses its power over us; servant—body waits at the foot of the hill, and the master—spirit worships upon the summit in the presence of the Lord. O that a hallowed season of divine communion may be vouchsafed to me this evening! The Lord knows that I need it very greatly. My graces languish, my corruptions rage, my faith is weak, my devotion is cold; all these are reasons why His healing hand should be laid upon me. His hand can cool the heat of my burning brow, and stay the tumult of my palpitating heart. That glorious right hand which molded the world can new-create my mind; the unwearied hand which bears the earth's huge pillars up can sustain my spirit; the loving hand which incloses all the saints can cherish me; and the mighty hand which breaketh in pieces the enemy can subdue my sins. Why should I not feel that hand touching me this evening? Come, my soul, address thy God with the potent plea, that Jesus' hands were pierced for thy redemption, and thou shalt surely feel that same hand upon thee which once touched Daniel and set him upon his knees that he might see visions of God.

Thy love is better than wine.
SONG OF SOLOMON 1:2

Nothing gives the believer so much joy as fellowship with Christ. He has enjoyment as others have in the common mercies of life, he can be glad both in God's gifts and God's works; but in all these separately, yea, and in all of them added together, he doth not find such substantial delight as in the matchless person of his Lord Jesus. He has wine which no vineyard on earth ever yielded; he has bread which all the cornfields of Egypt could never bring forth. Where can such sweetness be found as we have tasted in communion with our Beloved? In our esteem, the joys of earth are little better than husks for swine compared with Jesus, the heavenly manna. We would rather have one mouthful of Christ's love, and a sip of His fellowship, than a whole world full of carnal delights. What is the chaff to the wheat? What is the sparkling paste to the true diamond? What is a dream to the glorious reality? What is time's mirth, in its best trim, compared to our Lord Jesus in His most despised estate? If you know anything of the inner life, you will confess that our highest, purest, and most enduring joys must be the fruit of the tree of life which is in the midst of the Paradise of God. No spring yields such sweet water as that well of God which was digged with the soldier's spear. All earthly bliss is of the earth earthy, but the comforts of Christ's presence are like Himself, heavenly. We can review our communion with Jesus, and find no regrets of emptiness therein; there are no dregs in this wine, no dead flies in this ointment. The joy of the Lord is solid and enduring. Vanity hath not looked upon it, but discretion and prudence testify that it abideth the test of years, and is in time and in eternity worthy to be called "the only true delight." For nourishment, consolation, exhilaration, and refreshment, no wine can rival the love of Jesus. Let us drink to the full this evening.

I will help thee, saith the LORD.
ISAIAH 41:14

This morning let us hear the Lord Jesus speak to each one of us: "I will help thee." "It is but a small thing for Me, thy God, to help thee. Consider what I have done already. What! not help thee? Why, I bought thee with My blood. What! not help thee? I have died for thee; and if I have done the greater, will I not do the less? Help thee! It is the least thing I will ever do for thee; I have done more, and will do more. Before the world began I chose thee. I made the covenant for thee. I laid aside My glory and became a man for thee; I gave up My life for thee; and if I did all this, I will surely help thee now. In helping thee, I am giving thee what I have bought for thee already. If thou hadst need of a thousand times as much help, I would give it thee; thou requirest little compared with what I am ready to give. 'Tis much for thee to need, but it is nothing for me to bestow. 'Help thee?' Fear not! If there were an ant at the door of thy granary asking for help, it would not ruin thee to give him a handful of thy wheat; and thou art nothing but a tiny insect at the door of my all-sufficiency. 'I will help thee.' "

O my soul, is not this enough? Dost thou need more strength than the omnipotence of the united Trinity? Dost thou want more wisdom than exists in the Father, more love than displays itself in the Son, or more power than is manifest in the influences of the Spirit? Bring hither thine empty pitcher! Surely this well will fill it. Haste, gather up thy wants, and bring them here—thine emptiness, thy woes, thy needs. Behold, this river of God is full for thy supply; what canst thou desire beside? Go forth, my soul, in this thy might. The Eternal God is thine helper!

Fear not, I am with thee, oh, be not dismay'd!
I, I am thy God, and will still give thee aid.

We will remember thy love more than wine.
Song of Solomon 1:4

Jesus will not let His people forget His love. If all the love they have enjoyed should be forgotten, He will visit them with fresh love. "Do you forget My cross?" says He, "I will cause you to remember it; for at My table I will manifest Myself anew to you. Do you forget what I did for you in the council-chamber of eternity? I will remind you of it, for you shall need a counselor, and shall find Me ready at your call." Mothers do not let their children forget them. If the boy has gone to Australia, and does not write home, his mother writes—"Has John forgotten his mother?" Then there comes back a sweet epistle, which proves that the gentle reminder was not in vain. So is it with Jesus. He says to us, "Remember Me," and our response is, "We will remember Thy love." We will remember Thy love and its matchless history. It is ancient as the glory which Thou hadst with the Father before the world was. We remember, O Jesus, Thine eternal love when Thou didst become our Surety, and espouse us as Thy betrothed. We remember the love which suggested the sacrifice of Thyself, the love which, until the fullness of time, mused over that sacrifice, and long for the hour whereof in the volume of the book it was written of Thee, "Lo, I come." We remember Thy love, O Jesus! as it was manifest to us in Thy holy life, from the manger of Bethlehem to the garden of Gethsemane. We track Thee from the cradle to the grave—for every word and deed of Thine was love—and we rejoice in Thy love, which death did not exhaust; Thy love which shone resplendent in Thy resurrection. We remember that burning fire of love which will never let Thee hold Thy peace until Thy chosen ones be all safely housed, until Zion be glorified, and Jerusalem settled on her everlasting foundations of light and love in heaven.

I will mention the lovingkindnesses of the LORD,
and the praises of the LORD,
according to all that the LORD *hath bestowed on us.*
ISAIAH 63:7

And canst thou not do this? Are there no mercies which thou hast experienced? What though thou art gloomy now, canst thou forget that blessed hour when Jesus met thee, and said, "Come unto me"? Canst thou not remember that rapturous moment when He snapped thy fetters, dashed thy chains to the earth, and said, "I came to break thy bonds and set thee free"? Or if the love of thine espousals be forgotten, there must surely be some precious milestone along the road of life not quite grown over with moss, on which thou canst read a happy memorial of His mercy towards thee? What, didst thou never have a sickness like that which thou art suffering now, and did He not restore thee? Wert thou never poor before, and did He not supply thy wants? Wast thou never in straits before, and did He not deliver thee? Arise, go to the river of thine experience, and pull up a few bulrushes, and plait them into an ark, wherein thine infant—faith—may float safely on the stream. Forget not what thy God has done for thee; turn over the book of thy remembrance, and consider the days of old. Canst thou not remember the hill Mizar? Did the Lord never meet with thee at Hermon? Hast thou never climbed the Delectable Mountains? Hast thou never been helped in time of need? Nay, I know thou hast. Go back, then, a little way to the choice mercies of yesterday, and though all may be dark now, light up the lamps of the past, they shall glitter through the darkness, and thou shalt trust in the Lord till the day break and the shadows flee away. "Remember, O Lord, thy tender mercies and thy lovingkindnesses, for they have been ever of old."

Thy love to me was wonderful.
2 Samuel 1:26

Come, dear readers, let each one of us speak for himself of the wonderful love, not of Jonathan, but of Jesus. We will not relate what we have been told, but the things which we have tasted and handled—of the love of Christ. Thy love to me, O Jesus, was wonderful when I was a stranger wandering far from thee, fulfilling the desires of the flesh and of the mind. Thy love restrained me from committing the sin which is unto death and withheld me from self-destruction. Thy love held back the axe when Justice said, "Cut it down! why cumbereth it the ground?" Thy love drew me into the wilderness, stripped me there, and made me feel the guilt of my sin, and the burden of mine iniquity. Thy love spake thus comfortably to me when I was sore dismayed—"Come unto me, and I will give thee rest." Oh, how matchless Thy love when, in a moment, Thou didst wash my sins away and make my polluted soul, which was crimson with the blood of my nativity and black with the grime of my transgressions, to be white as the driven snow and pure as the finest wool. How Thou didst commend Thy love when Thou didst whisper in my ears, "I am thine and thou art Mine." Kind were those accents when thou saidst, "The Father Himself loveth you." And sweet the moments, passing sweet, when Thou declaredst to me "the love of the Spirit." Never shall my soul forget those chambers of fellowship where Thou has unveiled Thyself to me. Had Moses his cleft in the rock where he saw the train, the back parts of his God? We, too, have had our clefts in the rock where we have seen the full splendors of the Godhead in the person of Christ. Did David remember the tracks of the wild goat, the land of Jordan and the Hermonites? We, too, can remember spots to memory dear, equal to these in blessedness. Precious Lord Jesus, give us a fresh draught of Thy wondrous love to begin the month with. Amen.

Believer, look back through all thine experience, and think of the way whereby the Lord thy God has led thee in the wilderness, and how He hath fed and clothed thee every day—how He hath borne with thine ill manners—how He hath put up with all thy murmurings, and all thy longings after the flesh-pots of Egypt—how He has opened the rock to supply thee, and fed thee with manna that came down from heaven. Think of how His grace has been sufficient for thee in all thy troubles—how His blood has been a pardon to thee in all thy sins—how His rod and His staff have comforted thee. When thou hast thus looked back upon the love of the Lord, then let faith survey His love in the future, for remember that Christ's covenant and blood have something more in them than the past. He who has loved thee and pardoned thee shall never cease to love and pardon. He is Alpha, and He shall be Omega also: He is first, and He shall be last. Therefore, bethink thee, when thou shalt pass through the valley of the shadow of death, thou needest fear no evil, for He is with thee. When thou shalt stand in the cold floods of Jordan, thou needest not fear, for death cannot separate thee from His love; and when thou shalt come into the mysteries of eternity thou needest not tremble, "For I am persuaded, that neither death, nor life, nor angels, nor principalities, nor powers, nor things present, nor things to come, nor height, nor depth, nor any other creature, shall be able to separate us from the love of God, which is in Christ Jesus our Lord." Now, soul, is not thy love refreshed? Does not this make thee love Jesus? Doth not a flight through illimitable plains of the ether of love inflame thy heart and compel thee to delight thyself in the Lord thy God? Surely as we meditate on "the love of the Lord," our hearts burn within us, and we long to love Him more.

The Father sent the Son to be the Saviour of the world.
1 JOHN 4:14

It is a sweet thought that Jesus Christ did not come forth without His Father's permission, authority, consent, and assistance. He was sent of the Father, that He might be the Savior of men. We are too apt to forget that, while there are distinctions as to the persons in the Trinity, there are no distinctions of honor. We too frequently ascribe the honor of our salvation, or at least the depths of its benevolence, more to Jesus Christ than we do the Father. This is a very great mistake. What if Jesus came? Did not His Father send Him? If He spake wondrously, did not His Father pour grace into His lips, that He might be an able minister of the new covenant? He who knoweth the Father and the Son and the Holy Ghost as he should know them, never setteth one before another in his love; he sees them at Bethlehem, at Gethsemane, and on Calvary, all equally engaged in the work of salvation. O Christian, hast thou put thy confidence in the Man Christ Jesus? Hast thou placed thy reliance solely on Him? And art thou united with Him? Then believe that thou art united unto the God of heaven. Since to the Man Christ Jesus thou art brother and holdest closest fellowship, thou art linked thereby with God the Eternal, and "the Ancient of days" is thy Father and thy friend. Didst thou ever consider the depth of love in the heart of Jehovah, when God the Father equipped His Son for the great enterprise of mercy? If not, be this thy day's meditation. The Father sent Him! Contemplate that subject. Think how Jesus works what the Father wills. In the wounds of the dying Savior see the love of the great I AM. Let every thought of Jesus be also connected with the Eternal, ever—blessed God, for "It pleased the Lord to bruise Him; He hath put Him to grief."

Behold, what manner of love the Father hath bestowed upon
us, that we should be called the sons of God:
therefore the world knoweth us not, because it knew him not.
Beloved, now are we the sons of God.
1 John 3:1, 2

*B*ehold, what manner of love the Father hath bestowed upon us. Consider who we were, and what we feel ourselves to be even now when corruption is powerful in us, and you will wonder at our adoption. Yet we are called "the sons of God." What a high relationship is that of a son, and what privileges it brings! What care and tenderness the son expects from his father, and what love the father feels towards the son! But all that, and more than that, we now have through Christ. As for the temporary drawback of suffering with the elder brother, this we accept as an honour: "Therefore the world knoweth us not, because it knew him not." We are content to be unknown with Him in His humiliation, for we are to be exalted with Him. "Beloved, now are we the sons of God." That is easy to read, but it is not so easy to feel. How is it with your heart this morning? Are you in the lowest depths of sorrow? Does corruption rise within your spirit, and grace seem like a poor spark trampled under foot? Does your faith almost fail you? Fear not, it is neither your graces nor feelings on which you are to live: You must live simply by faith on Christ. With all these things against us, now—in the very depths of our sorrow, wherever we may be—now, as much in the valley as on the mountain, "Beloved, now are we the sons of God." "Ah, but," you say, "see how I am arrayed! my graces are not bright; my righteousness does not shine with apparent glory." But read the next: "It doth not yet appear what we shall be: but we know that, when he shall appear, we shall be like him." The Holy Spirit shall purify our minds, and divine power shall refine our bodies, then shall we see Him as He is.

There is therefore now no condemnation.
ROMANS 8:1

*C*ome, my soul, think thou of this. Believing in Jesus, thou art actually and effectually cleared from guilt; thou art led out of thy prison. Thou art no more in fetters as a bond-slave; thou art delivered now from the bondage of the law; thou art freed from sin, and canst walk at large as a freeman, thy Savior's blood has procured thy full discharge. Thou hast a right now to approach thy Father's throne. No flames of vengeance are there to scare thee now; no fiery sword; justice cannot smite the innocent. Thy disabilities are taken away: thou wast once unable to see thy Father's face: thou canst see it now. Thou couldst not speak with Him: but now thou hast access with boldness. Once there was a fear of hell upon thee; but thou hast no fear of it now, for how can there be punishment for the guiltless? He who believeth is not condemned and cannot be punished. And more than all, the privileges thou mightst have enjoyed, if thou hadst never sinned, are thine now that thou art justified. All the blessings which thou wouldst have had if thou hadst kept the law, and more, are thine, because Christ has kept it for thee. All the love and the acceptance which perfect obedience could have obtained of God belong to thee, because Christ was perfectly obedient on thy behalf and hath imputed all His merits to thy account, that thou mightst be exceeding rich through Him, who for thy sake became exceeding poor. Oh! how great the debt of love and gratitude thou owest to thy Saviour!

> *A debtor to mercy alone,*
> *Of covenant mercy I sing;*
> *Nor fear with Thy righteousness on,*
> *My person and offerings to bring:*
> *The terrors of law and of God,*
> *With me can have nothing to do;*
> *My Saviour's obedience and blood*
> *Hide all my transgressions from view.*

God, that comforteth those that are cast down.
2 CORINTHIANS 7:6

*A*nd who comforteth like Him? Go to some poor, melancholy, distressed child of God; tell him sweet promises, and whisper in his ear choice words of comfort; he is like the deaf adder, he listens not to the voice of the charmer, charm he never so wisely. He is drinking gall and wormwood, and comfort him as you may, it will be only a note or two of mournful resignation that you will get from him; you will bring forth no psalms of praise, no hallelujahs, no joyful sonnets. But let God come to His child, let Him lift up his countenance, and the mourner's eyes glisten with hope. Do you not hear him sing—

> *'Tis paradise, if Thou art here;*
> *If Thou depart, 'tis hell?*

You could not have cheered him: but the Lord has done it; "He is the God of all comfort." There is no balm in Gilead, but there is balm in God. There is no physician among the creatures, but the Creator is Jehovah-rophi. It is marvellous how one sweet word of God will make whole songs for Christians. One word of God is like a piece of gold, and the Christian is the goldbeater and can hammer that promise out for whole weeks. So, then, poor Christian, thou needest not sit down in despair. Go to the Comforter and ask Him to give thee consolation. Thou art a poor dry well. You have heard it said that when a pump is dry, you must pour water down it first of all, and then you will get water, and so, Christian, when thou art dry, go to God, ask Him to shed abroad His joy in thy heart, and then thy joy shall be full. Do not go to earthly acquaintances, for you will find them Job's comforters after all; but go first and foremost to thy "God, that comforteth those that are cast down," and you will soon say, "In the multitude of my thoughts within me thy comforts delight my soul."

I will never leave thee.
HEBREWS 13:5

No promise is of private interpretation. Whatever God has said to any one saint, He has said to all. When He opens a well for one, it is that all may drink. When He openeth a granary-door to give out food, there may be some one starving man who is the occasion of its being opened, but all hungry saints may come and feed too. Whether He gave the word to Abraham or to Moses, matters not, O believer; He has given it to thee as one of the covenanted seed. There is not a high blessing too lofty for thee, nor a wide mercy too extensive for thee. Lift up now thine eyes to the north and to the south, to the east and to the west, for all this is thine. Climb to Pisgah's top and view the utmost limit of the divine promise, for the land is all thine own. There is not a brook of living water of which thou mayst not drink. If the land floweth with milk and honey, eat the honey and drink the milk, for both are thine. Be thou bold to believe, for He hath said, "I will never leave thee, nor forsake thee." In this promise, God gives to His people everything. "I will never leave thee." Then no attribute of God can cease to be engaged for us. Is He mighty? He will show himself strong on the behalf of them that trust Him. Is He love? Then with lovingkindness will He have mercy upon us. Whatever attributes may compose the character of Deity, every one of them to its fullest extent shall be engaged on our side. To put everything in one, there is nothing you can want, there is nothing you can ask for, there is nothing you can need in time or in eternity, there is nothing living, nothing dying, there is nothing in this world, nothing in the next world, there is nothing now, nothing at the resurrection-morning, nothing in heaven which is not contained in this text—"I will never leave thee, nor forsake thee."

With lovingkindness have I drawn thee.
JEREMIAH 31:3

The thunders of the law and the terrors of judgment are all used to bring us to Christ; but the final victory is effected by lovingkindness. The prodigal set out to his father's house from a sense of need; but his father saw him a great way off and ran to meet him; so that the last steps he took towards his father's house were with the kiss still warm upon his cheek and the welcome still musical in his ears.

> *Law and terrors do but harden*
> *All the while they work alone;*
> *But a sense of blood-bought pardon*
> *Will dissolve a heart of stone.*

The Master came one night to the door and knocked with the iron hand of the law; the door shook and trembled upon its hinges; but the man piled every piece of furniture which he could find against the door, for he said, "I will not admit the man." The Master turned away, but by-and-by He came back, and with His own soft hand, using most that part where the nail had penetrated, He knocked again—oh, so softly and tenderly. This time the door did not shake, but, strange to say, it opened, and there upon his knees the once unwilling host was found rejoicing to receive his guest. "Come in, come in; Thou hast so knocked that my bowels are moved for Thee. I could not think of Thy pierced hand leaving its blood-mark on my door and of Thy going away houseless, 'Thy head filled with dew, and Thy locks with the drops of the night.' I yield, I yield, Thy love has won my heart." So in every case, lovingkindness wins the day. What Moses with the tablets of stone could never do, Christ does with His pierced hand. Such is the doctrine of effectual calling. Do I understand it experimentally? Can I say, "He drew me, and I followed on, glad to confess the voice divine"? If so, may He continue to draw me, till at last I shall sit down at the marriage supper of the Lamb.

My grace is sufficient for thee.
2 CORINTHIANS 12:9

If none of God's saints were poor and tried, we should not know half so well the consolations of divine grace. When we find the wanderer who has not where to lay his head, who yet can say, "Still will I trust in the Lord"; when we see the pauper starving on bread and water, who still glories in Jesus; when we see the bereaved widow overwhelmed in affliction and yet having faith in Christ, oh! what honor it reflects on the gospel. God's grace is illustrated and magnified in the poverty and trials of believers. Saints bear up under every discouragement, believing that all things work together for their good, and that out of apparent evils a real blessing shall ultimately spring—that their God will either work a deliverance for them speedily or most assuredly support them in the trouble, as long as He is pleased to keep them in it. This patience of the saints proves the power of divine grace. There is a lighthouse out at sea: It is a calm night—I cannot tell whether the edifice is firm; the tempest must rage about it, and then I shall know whether it will stand. So with the Spirit's work: If it were not on many occasions surrounded with tempestuous waters, we should not know that it was true and strong; if the winds did not blow upon it, we should not know how firm and secure it was. The masterworks of God are those men who stand in the midst of difficulties, stedfast, unmoveable—

> *Calm mid the bewildering cry,*
> *Confident of victory.*

He who would glorify his God must set his account upon meeting with many trials. No man can be illustrious before the Lord unless his conflicts be many. If then, yours be a much-tried path, rejoice in it, because you will the better show forth the all-sufficient grace of God. As for His failing you, never dream of it—hate the thought. The God who has been sufficient until now, should be trusted to the end.

Abide in me.
JOHN 15:4

Communion with Christ is a certain cure for every ill. Whether it be the wormwood of woe or the cloying surfeit of earthly delight, close fellowship with the Lord Jesus will take bitterness from the one and satiety from the other. Live near to Jesus, Christian, and it is a matter of secondary importance whether thou livest on the mountain of honor or in the valley of humiliation. Living near to Jesus, thou art covered with the wings of God, and underneath thee are the everlasting arms. Let nothing keep thee from that hallowed intercourse, which is the choice privilege of a soul wedded to the well-beloved. Be not content with an interview now and then, but seek always to retain His company, for only in His presence hast thou either comfort or safety. Jesus should not be unto us a friend who calls upon us now and then, but one with whom we walk evermore. Thou hast a difficult road before thee: see, O traveller to heaven, that thou go not without thy guide. thou hast to pass through the fiery furnace; enter it not unless, like Shadrach, Meshach, and Abednego, thou hast the Son of God to be thy companion. Thou hast to storm the Jericho of thine own corruptions: Attempt not the warfare until, like Joshua, thou hast seen the Captain of the Lord's host, with His sword drawn in His hand. Thou art to meet the Esau of thy many temptations: Meet Him not until at Jabbok's brook thou hast laid hold upon the angel and prevailed. In every case, in every condition, thou wilt need Jesus; but most of all, when the iron gates of death shall open to thee. Keep thou close to thy soul's Husband, lean thy head upon His bosom, ask to be refreshed with the spiced wine of His pomegranate, and thou shalt be found of Him at the last, without spot or wrinkle or any such thing. Seeing thou hast lived with Him, and lived in Him here, thou shalt abide with Him for ever.

Thou shalt be called, Sought out.
Isaiah 62:12

The surpassing grace of God is seen very clearly in that we were not only sought, but sought out. Men seek for a thing which is lost upon the floor of the house, but in such a case there is only seeking, not seeking out. The loss is more perplexing and the search more persevering when a thing is sought out. We were mingled with the mire: We were as when some precious piece of gold falls into the sewer, and men gather out and carefully inspect a mass of abominable filth and continue to stir and rake and search among the heap until the treasure is found. Or, to use another figure, we were lost in a labyrinth; we wandered hither and thither, and when mercy came after us with the gospel, it did not find us at the first coming, it had to search for us and seek us out; for we as lost sheep were so desperately lost and had wandered into such a strange country, that it did not seem possible that even the Good Shepherd should track our devious roamings. Glory be to unconquerable grace, we were sought out! No gloom could hide us, no filthiness could conceal us, we were found and brought home. Glory be to infinite love, God the Holy Spirit restored us!

The lives of some of God's people, if they could be written would fill us with holy astonishment. Strange and marvelous are the ways which God used in their case to find His own. Blessed be His name, He never relinquishes the search until the chosen are sought out effectually. They are not a people sought today and cast away tomorrow. Almightiness and wisdom combined will make no failures, they shall be called, "Sought out!" That any should be sought out is matchless grace, but that we should be sought out is grace beyond degree! We can find no reason for it but God's own sovereign love and can only lift up our heart in wonder and praise the Lord that this night we wear the name of "Sought out."

Be strong in the grace that is in Christ Jesus.
2 TIMOTHY 2:1

*C*hrist has grace without measure in Himself, but He hath not retained it for Himself. As the reservoir empties itself into the pipes, so hath Christ emptied out His grace for His people. "Of His fulness have all we received, and grace for grace." He seems only to have in order to dispense to us. He stands like the fountain, always flowing, but only running in order to supply the empty pitchers and the thirsty lips which draw nigh unto it. Like a tree, He bears sweet fruit, not to hang on boughs, but to be gathered by those who need. Grace, whether its work be to pardon, to cleanse, to preserve, to strengthen, to enlighten, to quicken, or to restore, is ever to be had from Him freely and without price; nor is there one form of the work of grace which He has not bestowed upon His people. As the blood of the body, though flowing from the heart, belongs equally to every member, so the influences of grace are the inheritance of every saint united to the Lamb; and herein there is a sweet communion between Christ and His Church, inasmuch as they both receive the same grace. Christ is the head upon which the oil is first poured; but the same oil runs to the very skirts of the garments, so that the meanest saint has an unction of the same costly moisture as that which fell upon the head. This is true communion when the sap of grace flows from the stem to the branch and when it is perceived that the stem itself is sustained by the very nourishment which feeds the branch. As we day by day receive grace from Jesus and more constantly recognize it as coming from Him, we shall behold Him in communion with us and enjoy the felicity of communion with Him. Let us make daily use of our riches and ever repair to Him as to our own Lord in covenant, taking from Him the supply of all we need with as much boldness as men take money from their own purse.

As the Father hath loved me, so have I loved you.
JOHN 15:9

As the Father loves the Son, in the same manner Jesus loves His people. What is that divine method? He loved Him without beginning, and thus Jesus loves His members. "I have loved thee with an everlasting love." You can trace the beginning of human affection; you can easily find the beginning of your love to Christ, but His love to us is a stream whose source is hidden in eternity. God the Father loves Jesus without any change. Christian, take this for your comfort, that there is no change in Jesus Christ's love to those who rest in Him. Yesterday you were on Tabor's top, and you said, "He loves me"; today you are in the valley of humiliation, but He loves you still the same. On the hill Mizar and among the Hermons, you heard His voice, which spake so sweetly with the turtle-notes of love; and now on the sea, or even in the sea, when all His waves and billows go over you, His heart is faithful to His ancient choice. The Father loves the Son without any end, and thus does the Son love His people. Saint, thou needest not fear the loosing of the silver cord, for His love for thee will never cease. Rest confident that even down to the grave Christ will go with you, and that up again from it He will be your guide to the celestial hills. Moreover, the Father loves the Son without any measure, and the same immeasurable love the Son bestows upon His chosen ones. The whole heart of Christ is dedicated to His people. He "loved us and gave himself for us." His is a love which passeth knowledge. Ah! we have indeed an immutable Saviour, a precious Saviour, one who loves without measure, without change, without beginning, and without end, even as the Father loves Him! There is much food here for those who know how to digest it. May the Holy Ghost lead us into its marrow and fatness!

My beloved.
SONG OF SOLOMON 2:8

This was a golden name which the ancient Church in her most joyous moments was wont to give to the Anointed of the Lord. When the time of the singing of birds was come, and the voice of the turtle was heard in her land, her love-note was sweeter than either, as she sang, "My beloved is mine, and I am his: he feedeth among the lilies." Ever in her song of songs doth she call Him by that delightful name, "My beloved!" Even in the long winter, when idolatry had withered the garden of the Lord, her prophets found space to lay aside the burden of the Lord for a little season, and to say, as Esaias did, "Now will I sing to my wellbeloved a song of my beloved touching his vineyard." Though the saints had never seen His face, though as yet He was not made flesh, nor had dwelt among us, nor had man beheld His glory, yet He was the consolation of Israel, the hope and joy of all the chosen, the "beloved" of all those who were upright before the Most High. We, in the summer days of the Church, are also wont to speak of Christ as the best beloved of our soul, and to feel that He is very precious, the "chiefest among ten thousand, and the altogether lovely." So true is it that the Church loves Jesus and claims Him as her beloved, that the apostle dares to defy the whole universe to separate her from the love of Christ, and declares that neither persecutions, distress, affliction, peril, or the sword have been able to do it; nay, he joyously boasts, "In all these things we are more than conquerors through him that loved us."

O that we knew more of Thee, Thou ever precious one!

My sole possession is Thy love;
In earth beneath, or heaven above,
I have no other store;
And though with fervent suit I pray,
And importune Thee day by day,
I ask Thee nothing more.

Husbands, love your wives,
even as Christ also loved the church.
EPHESIANS 5:25

What a golden example Christ gives to His disciples! Few masters could venture to say, "If you would practice my teaching, imitate my life"; but as the life of Jesus is the exact transcript of perfect virtue, He can point to Himself as the paragon of holiness, as well as the teacher of it. The Christian should take nothing short of Christ for his model. Under no circumstances ought we to be content, unless we reflect the grace which was in Him. As a husband, the Christian is to look upon the portrait of Christ Jesus, and he is to paint according to that copy. The true Christian is to be such a husband as Christ was to His church. The love of a husband is special. The Lord Jesus cherishes for the church a peculiar affection, which is set upon her above the rest of mankind: "I pray for them: I pray not for the world." The elect church is the favorite of heaven, the treasure of Christ, the crown of His head, the bracelet of His arm, the breastplate of His heart, the very center and core of His love. A husband should love his wife with a constant love, for thus Jesus loves His church. He does not vary in His affection. He may change in His display of affection, but the affection itself is still the same. A husband should love his wife with an enduring love, for nothing "shall be able to separate us from the love of God, which is in Christ Jesus our Lord." A true husband loves his wife with a hearty love, fervent and intense. It is not mere lip-service. Ah! beloved, what more could Christ have done in proof of His love than He has done? Jesus has a delighted love towards His spouse: He prizes her affection, and delights in her with sweet complacence. Believer, you wonder at Jesus' love; you admire it—are you imitating it? In your domestic relationships is the rule and measure of your love— "even as Christ loved the church"?

The love of Christ, which passeth knowledge.
EPHESIANS 3:19

The love of Christ in its sweetness, its fullness, its greatness, its faithfulness, passeth all human comprehension. Where shall language be found which shall describe His matchless, His unparalleled love towards the children of men? It is so vast and boundless that, as the swallow but skimmeth the water and diveth not into its depths, so all descriptive words but touch the surface, while depths immeasurable lie beneath. Well might the poet say,

"O love, thou fathomless abyss!"

For this love of Christ is indeed measureless and fathomless; none can attain unto it. Before we can have any right idea of the love of Jesus, we must understand His previous glory in its height of majesty, and His incarnation upon the earth in all its depths of shame. But who can tell us the majesty of Christ? When He was enthroned in the highest heavens He was very God of very God; by Him were the heavens made and all the hosts thereof. His own almighty arm upheld the spheres; the praises of cherubim and seraphim perpetually surrounded Him; the full chorus of the hallelujahs of the universe unceasingly flowed to the foot of His throne: He reigned supreme above all His creatures, God over all, blessed for ever. Who can tell His height of glory then? And who, on the other hand, can tell how low He descended? To be a man was something, to be a man of sorrows was far more; to bleed and die and suffer, these were much for Him who was the Son of God; but to suffer such unparalleled agony—to endure a death of shame and desertion by His Father, this is a depth of condescending love which the most inspired mind must utterly fail to fathom. Herein is love! and truly it is love that "passeth knowledge." O let this love fill our hearts with adoring gratitude and lead us to practical manifestations of its power.

For he hath made him to be sin for us, who knew no sin;
that we might be made the righteousness of God in him.
2 CORINTHIANS 5:21

Mourning Christian! why weepest thou? Art thou mourning over thine own corruptions? Look to thy perfect Lord, and remember, thou art complete in Him; thou art in God's sight as perfect as if thou hadst never sinned; nay, more than that, the Lord our Righteousness hath put a divine garment upon thee, so that thou hast more than the righteousness of man—thou hast the righteousness of God. O thou who art mourning by reason of inbred sin and depravity, remember, none of thy sins can condemn thee. Thou hast learned to hate sin; but thou hast learned also to know that sin is not thine—it was laid upon Christ's head. Thy standing is not in thyself—it is in Christ; thine acceptance is not in thyself, but in thy Lord; thou art as much accepted of God today, with all thy sinfulness, as thou wilt be when thou standest before His throne, free from all corruption. O, I beseech thee, lay hold on this precious thought, perfection in Christ! For thou art "complete in Him." With thy Saviour's garment on, thou art holy as the Holy one. "Who is he that condemneth? It is Christ that died, yea rather, that is risen again, who is even at the right hand of God, who also maketh intercession for us." Christian, let thy heart rejoice, for thou art "accepted in the beloved"—what hast thou to fear? Let thy face ever wear a smile; live near thy Master; live in the suburbs of the Celestial City; for soon, when thy time has come, thou shalt rise up where thy Jesus sits and reign at His right hand, even as He has overcome and has sat down at His Father's right hand; and all this because the divine Lord "was made to be sin for us, who knew no sin; that we might be made the righteousness of God in Him."

I will fear no evil: for thou art with me.
PSALM 23:4

*B*ehold, how independent of outward circumstances the Holy Ghost can make the Christian! What a bright light may shine within us when it is all dark without! How firm, how happy, how calm, how peaceful we may be, when the world shakes to and fro, and the pillars of the earth are removed! Even death itself, with all its terrible influences, has no power to suspend the music of a Christian's heart, but rather makes that music become more sweet, more clear, more heavenly, till the last kind act which death can do is to let the earthly strain melt into the heavenly chorus, the temporal joy into the eternal bliss! Let us have confidence, then, in the blessed Spirit's power to comfort us. Dear reader, are you looking forward to poverty? Fear not; the divine Spirit can give you, in your want, a greater plenty than the rich have in their abundance. You know not what joys may be stored up for you in the cottage around which grace will plant the roses of content. Are you conscious of a growing failure of your bodily powers? Do you expect to suffer long nights of languishing and days of pain? O be not sad! That bed may become a throne to you. You little know how every pang that shoots through your body may be a refining fire to consume your dross—a beam of glory to light up the secret parts of your soul. Are the eyes growing dim? Jesus will be your light. Do the ears fail you? Jesus' name will be your soul's best music, and His person your dear delight. Socrates used to say, "Philosophers can be happy without music"; and Christians can be happier than philosophers when all outward causes of rejoicing are withdrawn. In Thee, my God, my heart shall triumph, come what may of ills without! By Thy power, O blessed Spirit, my heart shall be exceeding glad, though all things should fail me here below.

The place, which is called Calvary.
LUKE 23:33

*T*he hill of comfort is the hill of Calvary; the house of consolation is built with the wood of the cross; the temple of heavenly blessing is founded upon the riven rock—riven by the spear which pierced His side. No scene in sacred history ever gladdens the soul like Calvary's tragedy.

> *Is it not strange, the darkest hour*
> *That ever dawned on sinful earth,*
> *Should touch the heart with softer power,*
> *For comfort, than an angel's mirth?*
> *That to the Cross the mourner's eye should turn,*
> *Sooner than where the stars of Bethlehem burn?*

Light springs from the midday-midnight of Golgotha, and every herb of the field blooms sweetly beneath the shadow of the once accursed tree. In that place of thirst, grace hath dug a fountain which ever gusheth with waters pure as crystal, each drop capable of alleviating the woes of mankind. You who have had your seasons of conflict, will confess that it was not at Olivet that you ever found comfort, not on the hill of Sinai, nor on Tabor; but Gethsemane, Gabbatha, and Golgotha have been a means of comfort to you. The bitter herbs of Gethsemane have often taken away the bitters of your life; the scourge of Gabbatha has often scourged away your cares; and the groans of Calvary yields us comfort rare and rich. We never should have known Christ's love in all its heights and depths if He had not died; nor could we guess the Father's deep affection if He had not given His Son to die. The common mercies we enjoy all sing of love, just as the sea-shell, when we put it to our ears, whispers of the deep sea whence it came; but if we desire to hear the ocean itself, we must not look at everyday blessings but at the transactions of the crucifixion. He who would know love, let him retire to Calvary and see the Man of sorrows die.

Look upon mine affliction and my pain;
and forgive all my sins.
PSALM 25:18

It is well for us when prayers about our sorrows are linked with pleas concerning our sins—when, being under God's hand, we are not wholly taken up with our pain, but remember our offences against God. It is well, also, to take both sorrow and sin to the same place. It was to God that David carried his sorrow: It was to God that David confessed his sin. Observe, then, we must take our sorrows to God. Even your little sorrows you may roll upon God, for He counteth the hairs of your head; and your great sorrows you may commit to Him, for He holdeth the ocean in the hollow of His hand. Go to Him, whatever your present trouble may be, and you shall find Him able and willing to relieve you. But we must take our sins to God, too. We must carry them to the cross, that the blood may fall upon them, to purge away their guilt, and to destroy their defiling power.

The special lesson of the text is this—that we are to go to the Lord with sorrows and with sins in the right spirit. Note that all David asks concerning his sorrow is, "Look upon mine affliction and my pain"; but the next petition is vastly more express, definite, decided, plain—"Forgive all my sins." Many sufferers would have put it, "Remove my affliction and my pain, and look at my sins." But David does not say so; he cries, "Lord, as for my affliction and my pain, I will not dictate to Thy wisdom. Lord, look at them, I will leave them to Thee, I should be glad to have my pain removed, but do as Thou wilt; but as for my sins, Lord, I know what I want with them; I must have them forgiven; I cannot endure to lie under their curse for a moment." A Christian counts sorrow lighter in the scale than sin; he can bear that his troubles should continue, but he cannot support the burden of his transgressions.

*Nay, in all these things we are more than conquerors
through him that loved us.*
ROMANS 8:37

We go to Christ for forgiveness and then too often look to the law for power to fight our sins. Paul thus rebukes us, "O foolish Galatians, who hath bewitched you, that ye should not obey the truth? This only would I learn of you, Received ye the Spirit by the works of the law, or by the hearing of faith? Are ye so foolish? having begun in the Spirit, are ye now made perfect by the flesh?" Take your sins to Christ's cross, for the old man can only be crucified there: We are crucified with Him. The only weapon to fight sin with is the spear which pierced the side of Jesus. To give an illustration—you want to overcome an angry temper, how do you go to work? It is very possible you have never tried the right way of going to Jesus with it. How did I get salvation? I came to Jesus just as I was, and I trusted Him to save me. I must kill my angry temper in the same way? It is the only way in which I can ever kill it. I must go to the cross with it and say to Jesus, "Lord, I trust Thee to deliver me from it." This is the only way to give it a deathblow. Are you covetous? Do you feel the world entangle you? You may struggle against this evil so long as you please, but if it be your besetting sin, you will never be delivered from it in any way but by the blood of Jesus. Take it to Christ. Tell Him, "Lord, I have trusted Thee, and Thy name is Jesus, for Thou dost save Thy people from their sins; Lord, this is one of my sins; save me from it!" Ordinances are nothing without Christ as a means of mortification. Your prayers and your repentances and your tears—the whole of them put together—are worth nothing apart from Him. "None but Jesus can do helpless sinners good"; or helpless saints, either. You must be conquerors through Him who hath loved you, if conquerors at all. Our laurels must grow among His olives in Gethsemane

If any man hear my voice, and open the door,
I will come in to him.
REVELATION 3:20

*W*hat is your desire this evening? Is it set upon heavenly things? Do you long to enjoy the high doctrine of eternal love? Do you desire liberty in very close communion with God? Do you aspire to know the heights and depths and lengths and breadths? Then you must draw near to Jesus; you must get a clear sight of Him in His preciousness and completeness: you must view Him in His work, in His offices, in His person. He who understands Christ, receives an anointing from the Holy One, by which He knows all things. Christ is the great master-key of all the chambers of God: There is no treasure-house of God which will not open and yield up all its wealth to the soul that lives near to Jesus. Are you saying, "O that He would dwell in my bosom?" "Would that He would make my heart His dwelling-place for ever?" Open the door, Beloved, and He will come into your souls. He has long been knocking, and all with this object, that He may sup with you, and you with Him. He sups with you because you find the house or the heart, and you with Him because He brings the provision. He could not sup with you if it were not in your heart, you finding the house; nor could you sup with Him, for you have a bare cupboard, if He did not bring provision with Him. Fling wide, then, the portals of your soul. He will come with that love which you long to feel; He will come with that joy into which you cannot work your poor depressed spirit; He will bring the peace which now you have not; He will come with His flagons of wine and sweet apples of love, and cheer you till you have no other sickness but that of "love o'erpowering, love divine." Only open the door to Him, drive out His enemies, give Him the keys of your heart, and He will dwell there for ever. Oh, wondrous love, that brings such a guest to dwell in such a heart!

The LORD taketh pleasure in his people.
PSALM 149:4

How comprehensive is the love of Jesus! There is no part of His people's interests which He does not consider, and there is nothing which concerns their welfare which is not important to Him. Not merely does He think of you, Believer, as an immortal being, but as a mortal being, too. Do not deny it or doubt it: "The very hairs of your head are all numbered." "The steps of a good man are ordered by the Lord: and he delighteth in his way." It were a sad thing for us if this mantle of love did not cover all our concerns, for what mischief might be wrought to us in that part of our business which did not come under our gracious Lord's inspection! Believer, rest assured that the heart of Jesus cares about your meaner affairs. The breadth of His tender love is such that you may resort to Him in all matters; for in all your afflictions He is afflicted, and like as a father pitieth his children, so doth He pity you. The meanest interests of all His saints are all borne upon the broad bosom of the Son of God. Oh, what a heart is His, that doth not merely comprehend the persons of His people, but comprehends also the diverse and innumerable concerns of all those persons! Dost thou think, O Christian, that thou canst measure the love of Christ? Think of what His love has brought thee—justification, adoption, sanctification, eternal life! The riches of His goodness are unsearchable; thou shalt never be able to tell them out or even conceive them. Oh, the breadth of the love of Christ! Shall such a love as this have half our hearts? Shall it have a cold love in return? Shall Jesus' marvelous lovingkindness and tender care meet with but faint response and tardy acknowledgment? O my soul, tune thy harp to a glad song of thanksgiving! Go to thy rest rejoicing, for thou art no desolate wanderer, but a beloved child, watched over, cared for, supplied, and defended by thy Lord.

How precious also are thy thoughts unto me, O God.
PSALM 139:17

Divine omniscience affords no comfort to the ungodly mind, but to the child of God it overflows with consolation. God is always thinking upon us, never turns aside His mind from us, has us always before His eyes; and this is precisely as we would have it, for it would be dreadful to exist for a moment beyond the observation of our heavenly Father. His thoughts are always tender, loving, wise, prudent, far-reaching, and they bring to us countless benefits: Hence it is a choice delight to remember them. The Lord always did think upon His people: Hence their election and the covenant of grace by which their salvation is secured. He always will think upon them: Hence their final perseverance by which they shall be brought safely to their final rest. In all our wanderings the watchful glance of the Eternal Watcher is evermore fixed upon us—we never roam beyond the Shepherd's eye. In our sorrows He observes us incessantly, and not a pang escapes Him; in our toils He marks all our weariness, and writes in His book all the struggles of His faithful ones. These thoughts of the Lord encompass us in all our paths and penetrate the innermost region of our being. Not a nerve or tissue, valve or vessel, of our bodily organization is uncared for; all the littles of our little world are thought upon by the great God.

Dear reader, is this precious to you? then hold to it. Never be led astray by those philosophic fools who preach up an impersonal God and talk of self-existent, self-governing matter. The Lord liveth and thinketh upon us, this is a truth far too precious for us to be lightly robbed of it. The notice of a nobleman is valued so highly that he who has it counts his fortune made; but what is it to be thought of by the King of kings! If the Lord thinketh upon us, all is well, and we may rejoice evermore.

A very present help.
PSALM 46:1

*C*ovenant blessings are not meant to be looked at only but to be appropriated. Even our Lord Jesus is given to us for our present use. Believer, thou dost not make use of Christ as thou oughtest to do. When thou art in trouble, why dost thou not tell Him all thy grief? Has He not a sympathizing heart, and can He not comfort and relieve thee? No, thou art going about to all thy friends, save thy best Friend, and telling thy tale everywhere except into the bosom of thy Lord. Art thou burdened with this day's sins? Here is a fountain filled with blood: Use it, Saint, use it. Has a sense of guilt returned upon thee? The pardoning grace of Jesus may be proved again and again. Come to Him at once for cleansing. Dost thou deplore thy weakness? He is thy strength: Why not lean upon Him? Dost thou feel naked? Come hither, Soul; put on the robe of Jesus' righteousness. Stand not looking at it, but wear it. Strip off thine own righteousness and thine own fears, too: put on the fair white linen, for it was meant to wear. Dost thou feel thyself sick? Pull the night-bell of prayer, and call up the Beloved Physician! He will give the cordial that will revive thee. Thou art poor, but then thou hast "a kinsman, a mighty man of wealth." What! wilt thou not go to Him and ask Him to give thee of His abundance, when He has given thee this promise, that thou shalt be joint heir with Him, and has made over all that He is and all that He has to be thine? There is nothing Christ dislikes more than for His people to make a show-thing of Him and not to use Him. He loves to be employed by us. The more burdens we put on His shoulders, the more precious will He be to us.

Let us be simple with Him, then,
  Not backward, stiff, or cold,
As though our Bethlehem could be
  What Sinai was of old.

I will be their God,
and they shall be my people.
2 CORINTHIANS 6:16

*W*hat a sweet title: "My people!" What a cheering revelation: "Their God!" How much of meaning is couched in those two words, "My people!" Here is speciality. The whole world is God's; the heaven, even the heaven of heavens is the Lord's, and He reigneth among the children of men; but of those whom He hath chosen, whom He hath purchased to Himself, He saith what He saith not of others—"My people." In this word there is the idea of proprietorship. In a special manner the "Lord's portion is his people; Jacob is the lot of his inheritance." All the nations upon earth are His; the whole world is in His power; yet are His people, His chosen, more especially His possession; for He has done more for them than others; He has bought them with His blood; He has brought them nigh to Himself; He has set His great heart upon them; He has loved them with an everlasting love, a love which many waters cannot quench, and which the revolutions of time shall never suffice in the least degree to diminish. Dear friends, can you, by faith, see yourselves in that number? Can you look up to heaven and say, "My Lord and my God: mine by that sweet relationship which entitles me to call Thee Father; mine by that hallowed fellowship which I delight to hold with Thee when Thou art pleased to manifest Thyself unto me as Thou dost not unto the world?" Canst thou read the Book of Inspiration and find there the indentures of thy salvation? Canst thou read thy title writ in precious blood? Canst thou, by humble faith, lay hold of Jesus' garments and say, "My Christ"? If thou canst, then God saith of thee, and of others like thee, "My people"; for, if God be your God and Christ your Christ, the Lord has a special, peculiar favor to you; you are the object of His choice, accepted in His beloved Son.

Who hath blessed us with all spiritual blessings.
EPHESIANS 1:3

*A*ll the goodness of the past, the present, and the future, Christ bestows upon His people. In the mysterious ages of the past the Lord Jesus was His Father's first elect, and in His election He gave us an interest, for we were chosen in Him from before the foundation of the world. He had from all eternity the prerogatives of Sonship, as His Father's only-begotten and well-beloved Son, and He has, in the riches of His grace, by adoption and regeneration, elevated us to sonship also, so that to us He has given "power to become the sons of God." The eternal covenant, based upon suretiship and confirmed by oath, is ours, for our strong consolation and security. In the everlasting settlements of predestinating wisdom and omnipotent decree, the eye of the Lord Jesus was ever fixed on us; and we may rest assured that in the whole roll of destiny there is not a line which militates against the interests of His redeemed. The great betrothal of the Prince of Glory is ours, for it is to us that He is affianced, as the sacred nuptials shall ere long declare to an assembled universe. The marvelous incarnation of the God of heaven, with all the amazing condescension and humiliation which attended it, is ours. The bloody sweat, the scourge, the cross, are ours for ever. Whatever blissful consequences flow from perfect obedience, finished atonement, resurrection, ascension, or intercession, all are ours by His own gift. Upon His breastplate He is now bearing our names; and in His authoritative pleadings at the throne He remembers our persons and pleads our cause. His dominion over principalities and powers, and His absolute majesty in heaven, He employs for the benefit of them who trust in Him. His high estate is as much at our service as was His condition of abasement. He who gave Himself for us in the depths of woe and death, doth not withdraw the grant now that He is enthroned in the highest heavens.

I am with you alway.
MATTHEW 28:20

It is well there is One who is ever the same and who is ever with us. It is well there is one stable rock amidst the billows of the sea of life. O my soul, set not thine affections upon rusting, moth-eaten, decaying treasures, but set thine heart upon Him who abides forever faithful to thee. Build not thine house upon the moving quicksands of a deceitful world, but found thy hopes upon this rock, which, amid descending rain and roaring floods, shall stand immovably secure. My soul, I charge thee, lay up thy treasure in the only secure cabinet; store thy jewels where thou canst never lose them. Put thine all in Christ; set all thine affections on His person, all thy hope in His merit, all thy trust in His efficacious blood, all thy joy in His presence, and so thou mayest laugh at loss and defy destruction. Remember that all the flowers in the world's garden fade by turns, and the day cometh when nothing will be left but the black, cold earth. Death's black extinguisher must soon put out thy candle. Oh! how sweet to have sunlight when the candle is gone! The dark flood must soon roll between thee and all thou hast; then wed thine heart to Him who will never leave thee; trust thyself with Him who will go with thee through the black and surging current of death's stream and who will land thee safely on the celestial shore and make thee sit with Him in heavenly places for ever. Go, sorrowing son of affliction, tell thy secrets to the Friend who sticketh closer than a brother. Trust all thy concerns with Him who never can be taken from thee, who will never leave thee, and who will never let thee leave Him, even "Jesus Christ, the same yesterday, and to day, and for ever." "Lo, I am with you alway" is enough for my soul to live upon, let who will forsake me.

He shall gather the lambs with his arm,
and carry them in his bosom.
Isaiah 40:11

Who is He of whom such gracious words are spoken? He is the Good Shepherd. Why doth He carry the lambs in His bosom? Because He hath a tender heart, and any weakness at once melts His heart. The sighs, the ignorance, the feebleness of the little ones of His flock draw forth His compassion. It is His office, as a faithful High Priest, to consider the weak. Besides, He purchased them with blood, they are His property: He must and will care for that which cost Him so dear. Then He is responsible for each lamb, bound by covenant engagements not to lose one. Moreover, they are all a part of His glory and reward.

But how may we understand the expression, "He will carry them"? Sometimes He carries them by not permitting them to endure much trial. Providence deals tenderly with them. Often they are "carried" by being filled with an unusual degree of love, so that they bear up and stand fast. Though their knowledge may not be deep, they have great sweetness in what they do know. Frequently He "carries" them by giving them a very simple faith, which takes the promise just as it stands and believingly runs with every trouble straight to Jesus. The simplicity of their faith gives them an unusual degree of confidence, which carries them above the world.

"He carries the lambs in His bosom." Here is boundless affection. Would He put them in His bosom if He did not love them much? Here is tender nearness: So near are they, that they could not possibly be nearer. Here is hallowed familiarity: There are precious love-passages between Christ and His weak ones. Here is perfect safety: In His bosom who can hurt them? They must hurt the Shepherd first. Here is perfect rest and sweetest comfort. Surely we are not sufficiently sensible of the infinite tenderness of Jesus!

Who giveth us richly all things to enjoy.
1 TIMOTHY 6:17

*O*ur Lord Jesus is ever giving and does not for a solitary instant withdraw His hand. As long as there is a vessel of grace not yet full to the brim, the oil shall not be stayed. He is a sun ever-shining; He is manna always falling round the camp; He is a rock in the desert, ever sending out streams of life from His smitten side; the rain of His grace is always dropping; the river of His bounty is ever-flowing, and the well-spring of His love is constantly overflowing. As the King can never die, so His grace can never fail. Daily we pluck His fruit, and daily His branches bend down to our hand with a fresh store of mercy. There are seven feast-days in His weeks, and as many as are the days, so many are the banquets in His years. Who has ever returned from His door unblessed? Who has ever risen from His table unsatisfied, or from His bosom unemparadised? His mercies are new every morning and fresh every evening. Who can know the number of His benefits or recount the list of His bounties? Every sand which drops from the glass of time is but the tardy follower of a myriad of mercies. The wings of our hours are covered with the silver of His kindness and with the yellow gold of His affection. The river of time bears from the mountains of eternity the golden sands of His favor. The countless stars are but as the standard bearers of a more innumerable host of blessings. Who can count the dust of the benefits which He bestows on Jacob or tell the number of the fourth part of His mercies towards Israel? How shall my soul extol Him who daily loadeth us with benefits and who crowneth us with loving-kindness? O that my praise could be as ceaseless as His bounty! O miserable tongue, how canst thou be silent? Wake up, I pray thee, lest I call thee no more my glory, but my shame. "Awake, psaltery and harp: I myself will awake right early."

Marvellous lovingkindness.
PSALM 17:7

When we give our hearts with our alms, we give well, but we must often plead to a failure in this respect. Not so our Master and our Lord. His favors are always performed with the love of His heart. He does not send to us the cold meat and the broken pieces from the table of His luxury, but He dips our morsel in His own dish, and seasons our provisions with the spices of His fragrant affections. When He puts the golden tokens of His grace into our palms, He accompanies the gift with such a warm pressure of our hand, that the manner of His giving is as precious as the boon itself. He will come into our houses upon His errands of kindness, and He will not act as some austere visitors do in the poor man's cottage, but He sits by our side, not despising our poverty, nor blaming our weakness. Beloved, with what smiles does He speak! What golden sentences drop from His gracious lips! What embraces of affection does He bestow upon us! If He had but given us farthings, the way of His giving would have gilded them; but as it is, the costly alms are set in a golden basket by His pleasant carriage. It is impossible to doubt the sincerity of His charity, for there is a bleeding heart stamped upon the face of all His benefactions. He giveth liberally and upbraideth not. Not one hint that we are burdensome to Him; not one cold look for His poor pensioners; but He rejoices in His mercy and presses us to His bosom while He is pouring out His life for us. There is a fragrance in His spikenard which nothing but His heart could produce; there is a sweetness in His honeycomb which could not be in it unless the very essence of His soul's affection had been mingled with it. Oh! the rare communion which such singular heartiness effecteth! May we continually taste and know the blessedness of it!

Blessed be God, which hath not turned away my prayer.
PSALM 66:20

In looking back upon the character of our prayers, if we do it honestly, we shall be filled with wonder that God has ever answered them. There may be some who think their prayers worthy of acceptance—as the Pharisee did; but the true Christian, in a more enlightened retrospect, weeps over his prayers, and if he could retrace his steps he would desire to pray more earnestly. Remember, Christian, how cold thy prayers have been. When in thy closet thou shouldst have wrestled as Jacob did; but instead thereof, thy petitions have been faint and few—far removed from that humble, believing, persevering faith, which cries, "I will not let thee go except thou bless me." Yet, wonderful to say, God has heard these cold prayers of thine, and not only heard, but answered them. Reflect also, how infrequent have been thy prayers, unless thou hast been in trouble, and then thou hast gone often to the mercy-seat: But when deliverance has come, where has been thy constant supplication? Yet, notwithstanding thou hast ceased to pray as once thou didst, God has not ceased to bless. When thou hast neglected the mercy-seat, God has not deserted it, but the bright light of the Shekinah has always been visible between the wings of the cherubim. Oh! it is marvelous that the Lord should regard those intermittent spasms of importunity which come and go with our necessities. What a God is He thus to hear the prayers of those who come to Him when they have pressing wants, but neglect Him when they have received a mercy; who approach Him when they are forced to come, but who almost forget to address Him when mercies are plentiful and sorrows are few. Let His gracious kindness in hearing such prayers touch our hearts, so that we may henceforth be found "Praying always with all prayer and supplication in the Spirit."

Whom he justified, them he also glorified.
ROMANS 8:30

*H*ere is a precious truth for thee, Believer. Thou mayest be poor or in suffering or unknown, but for thine encouragement take a review of thy "calling" and the consequences that flow from it and especially that blessed result here spoken of. As surely as thou art God's child today, so surely shall all thy trials soon be at an end, and thou shalt be rich to all the intents of bliss. Wait awhile, and that weary head shall wear the crown of glory, and that hand of labor shall grasp the palm-branch of victory. Lament not thy troubles, but rather rejoice that ere long thou wilt be where "there shall be neither sorrow, nor crying, neither shall there be any more pain." The chariots of fire are at thy door, and a moment will suffice to bear thee to the glorified. The everlasting song is almost on thy lip. The portals of heaven stand open for thee. Think not that thou canst fail of entering into rest. If He hath called thee, nothing can divide thee from His love. Distress cannot sever the bond; the fire of persecution cannot burn the link; the hammer of hell cannot break the chain. Thou art secure; that voice which called thee at first, shall call thee yet again from earth to heaven, from death's dark gloom to immortality's unuttered splendors. Rest assured, the heart of Him who has justified thee beats with infinite love towards thee. Thou shalt soon be with the glorified, where thy portion is; thou art only waiting here to be made meet for the inheritance, and that done, the wings of angels shall waft thee far away, to the mount of peace and joy and blessedness, where,

> *Far from a world of grief and sin,*
> *With God eternally shut in,*
> *thou shalt rest for ever and ever.*

f the young man in the gospel used this title in speaking to our Lord, how much more fitly may I thus address Him! He is indeed my Master in both senses, a ruling Master and a teaching Master. I delight to run upon His errands and to sit at His feet. I am both His servant and His disciple and count it my highest honour to own the double character. If He should ask me why I call Him "good," I should have a ready answer. It is true that "there is none good but one, that is, God," but then He is God, and all the goodness of Deity shines forth in Him. In my experience, I have found Him good, so good, indeed, that all the good I have has come to me through Him. He was good to me when I was dead in sin, for He raised me by His Spirit's power; He has been good to me in all my needs, trials, struggles, and sorrows. Never could there be a better Master, for His service is freedom, His rule is love: I wish I were one thousandth part as good a servant. When He teaches me as my Rabbi, He is unspeakably good, His doctrine is divine, His manner is condescending, His spirit is gentleness itself. No error mingles with His instruction—pure is the golden truth which He brings forth, and all His teachings lead to goodness, sanctifying as well as edifying the disciple. Angels find Him a good Master and delight to pay their homage at His footstool. The ancient saints proved Him to be a good Master, and each of them rejoiced to sing, "I am Thy servant, O Lord!" My own humble testimony must certainly be to the same effect. I will bear this witness before my friends and neighbors, for possibly they may be led by my testimony to seek my Lord Jesus as their Master. O that they would do so! They would never repent so wise a deed. If they would but take His easy yoke, they would find themselves in so royal a service that they would enlist in it for ever.

*H*ow sweet it is to behold the Savior communing with His own beloved people! There can be nothing more delightful than, by the Divine Spirit, to be led into this fertile field of delight. Let the mind for an instant consider the history of the Redeemer's love, and a thousand enchanting acts of affection will suggest themselves, all of which have had for their design the weaving of the heart into Christ, and the intertwisting of the thoughts and emotions of the renewed soul with the mind of Jesus. When we meditate upon this amazing love, and behold the all-glorious Kinsman of the Church endowing her with all His ancient wealth, our souls may well faint for joy. Who is he that can endure such a weight of love? That partial sense of it, which the Holy Spirit is sometimes pleased to afford, is more than the soul can contain; how transporting must be a complete view of it! When the soul shall have understanding to discern all the Savior's gifts, wisdom wherewith to estimate them, and time in which to meditate upon them, such as the world to come will afford us, we shall then commune with Jesus in a nearer manner than at present. But who can imagine the sweetness of such fellowship? It must be one of the things which have not entered into the heart of man, but which God hath prepared for them that love Him. Oh, to burst open the door of our Joseph's granaries and see the plenty which He hath stored up for us! This will overwhelm us with love. By faith we see, as in a glass darkly, the reflected image of His unbounded treasures, but when we shall actually see the heavenly things themselves, with our own eyes, how deep will be the stream of fellowship in which our soul shall bathe itself! Till then our loudest sonnets shall be reserved for our loving benefactor, Jesus Christ our Lord, whose love to us is wonderful, passing the love of women.

The LORD hath done great things for us, whereof we are glad.
PSALM 126:3

*S*ome Christians are sadly prone to look on the dark side of everything and to dwell more upon what they have gone through than upon what God has done for them. Ask for their impression of the Christian life, and they will describe their continual conflicts, their deep afflictions, their sad adversities, and the sinfulness of their hearts, yet with scarcely any allusion to the mercy and help which God has vouchsafed them. But a Christian whose soul is in a healthy state, will come forward joyously, and say, "I will speak, not about myself, but to the honor of my God. He hath brought me up out of an horrible pit and out of the miry clay and set my feet upon a rock and established my goings: and he hath put a new song in my mouth, even praise unto our God. The Lord hath done great things for me, whereof I am glad." Such an abstract of experience as this is the very best that any child of God can present. It is true that we endure trials, but it is just as true that we are delivered out of them. It is true that we have our corruptions, and mournfully do we know this, but it is quite as true that we have an all-sufficient Savior, who overcomes these corruptions, and delivers us from their dominion. In looking back, it would be wrong to deny that we have been in the Slough of Despond and have crept along the Valley of Humiliation, but it would be equally wicked to forget that we have been through them safely and profitably; we have not remained in them, thanks to our Almighty Helper and Leader, who has brought us "out into a wealthy place." The deeper our troubles, the louder our thanks to God, who has led us through all and preserved us until now. Our griefs cannot mar the melody of our praise, we reckon them to be the bass part of our life's song, "He hath done great things for us, whereof we are glad."

There is no light in the planet but that which proceedeth from the sun; and there is no true love to Jesus in the heart but that which cometh from the Lord Jesus Himself. From this overflowing fountain of the infinite love of God, all our love to God must spring. This must ever be a great and certain truth, that we love Him for no other reason than because He first loved us. Our love to Him is the fair offspring of His love to us. Cold admiration, when studying the works of God, anyone may have, but the warmth of love can only be kindled in the heart by God's Spirit. How great the wonder that such as we should ever have been brought to love Jesus at all! How marvelous that when we had rebelled against Him, He should, by a display of such amazing love, seek to draw us back. No! never should we have had a grain of love towards God unless it had been sown in us by the sweet seed of His love to us. Love, then, has for its parent the love of God shed abroad in the heart: But after it is thus divinely born, it must be divinely nourished. Love is an exotic; it is not a plant which will flourish naturally in human soil, it must be watered from above. Love to Jesus is a flower of a delicate nature, and if it received no nourishment but that which could be drawn from the rock of our hearts it would soon wither. As love comes from heaven, so it must feed on heavenly bread. It cannot exist in the wilderness unless it be fed by manna from on high. Love must feed on love. The very soul and life of our love to God is His love to us.

> *I love Thee, Lord, but with no love of mine,*
> *For I have none to give;*
> *I love Thee, Lord; but all the love is Thine,*
> *For by Thy love I live.*
> *I am as nothing, and rejoice to be*
> *Emptied, and lost, and swallowed up in Thee.*

Whosoever will, let him take the water of life freely.
REVELATION 22:17

*J*esus says, "take freely." He wants no payment or preparation. He seeks no recommendation from our virtuous emotions. If you have no good feelings, if you be but willing, you are invited; therefore come! You have no belief and no repentance—come to Him, and He will give them to you. Come just as you are, and take "freely," without money and without price. He gives Himself to needy ones. The drinking fountains at the corners of our streets are valuable institutions; and we can hardly imagine anyone so foolish as to feel for his purse, when he stands before one of them, and to cry, "I cannot drink because I have not five pounds in my pocket." However poor the man is, there is the fountain, and just as he is he may drink of it. Thirsty passengers, as they go by, whether they are dressed in fustian or in broadcloth, do not look for any warrant for drinking; its being there is their warrant for taking its water freely. The liberality of some good friends has put the refreshing crystal there, and we take it and ask no questions. Perhaps the only persons who need go thirsty through the street where there is a drinking fountain are the fine ladies and gentlemen who are in their carriages. They are very thirsty, but cannot think of being so vulgar as to get out to drink. It would demean them, they think, to drink at a common drinking fountain: So they ride by with parched lips. Oh, how many there are who are rich in their own good works and cannot therefore come to Christ! "I will not be saved," they say, "in the same way as the harlot or the swearer." What! go to heaven in the same way as a chimney sweep. Is there no pathway to glory but the path which led the thief there? I will not be saved that way. Such proud boasters must remain without the living water; but, "whosoever will, let Him take the water of life freely."

The LORD is my light and my salvation; whom shall I fear?
the LORD is the strength of my life; of whom shall I be afraid?
PSALM 27:1

"The Lord is my light and my salvation." Here is personal interest, "my light," "my salvation"; the soul is assured of it, and therefore declares it boldly. Into the soul at the new birth divine light is poured as the precursor of salvation; where there is not enough light to reveal our own darkness and to make us long for the Lord Jesus, there is no evidence of salvation. After conversion our God is our joy, comfort, guide, teacher, and in every sense, our light: He is light within, light around, light reflected from us, and light to be revealed to us. Note, it is not said merely that the Lord gives light, but that He is light; nor that He gives salvation, but that He is salvation; he, then, who by faith has laid hold upon God, has all covenant blessings in His possession. This being made sure as a fact, the argument drawn from it is put in the form of a question, "Whom shall I fear?" A question which is its own answer. The powers of darkness are not to be feared, for the Lord, our light, destroys them; and the damnation of hell is not to be dreaded by us, for the Lord is our salvation. This is a very different challenge from that of boastful Goliath, for it rests, not upon the conceited vigor of an arm of flesh, but upon the real power of the omnipotent I AM. "The Lord is the strength of my life." Here is a third glowing epithet, to show that the writer's hope was fastened with a threefold cord which could not be broken. We may well accumulate terms of praise where the Lord lavishes deeds of grace. Our life derives all its strength from God; and if He deigns to make us strong, we cannot be weakened by all the machinations of the adversary. "Of whom shall I be afraid?" The bold question looks into the future as well as the present. "If God be for us," who can be against us, either now or in time to come?

The foundation of God standeth sure.
2 TIMOTHY 2:19

The foundation upon which our faith rests is this, that "God was in Christ, reconciling the world unto himself, not imputing their trespasses unto them." The great fact on which genuine faith relies is, that "the Word was made flesh and dwelt among us," and that "Christ also hath suffered for sin, the just for the unjust, that he might bring us to God"; "Who himself bare our sins in his own body on the tree"; "For the chastisement of our peace was upon him, and by his stripes we are healed." In one word, the great pillar of the Christian's hope is substitution. The vicarious sacrifice of Christ for the guilty, Christ being made sin for us that we might be made the righteousness of God in Him, Christ offering up a true and proper expiatory and substitutionary sacrifice in the room, place, and stead of as many as the Father gave Him, who are known to God by name, and are recognised in their own hearts by their trusting in Jesus—this is the cardinal fact of the gospel. If this foundation were removed, what could we do? But it standeth firm as the throne of God. We know it; we rest on it; we rejoice in it; and our delight is to hold it, to meditate upon it, and to proclaim it, while we desire to be actuated and moved by gratitude for it in every part of our life and conversation. In these days a direct attack is made upon the doctrine of the atonement. Men cannot bear substitution. They gnash their teeth at the thought of the Lamb of God bearing the sin of man. But we, who know by experience the preciousness of this truth, will proclaim it in defiance of them confidently and unceasingly. We will neither dilute it nor change it nor fritter it away in any shape or fashion. It shall still be Christ, a positive substitute, bearing human guilt and suffering in the stead of men. We cannot, dare not, give it up, for it is our life, and despite every controversy we feel that "nevertheless the foundation of God standeth sure."

And the glory which thou gavest me I have given them.
JOHN 17:22

*B*ehold the superlative liberality of the Lord Jesus, for He hath given us His all. Although a tithe of His possessions would have made a universe of angels rich beyond all thought, yet was He not content until He had given us all that He had. It would have been surprising grace if He had allowed us to eat the crumbs of His bounty beneath the table of His mercy; but He will do nothing by halves, He makes us sit with Him and share the feast. Had He given us some small pension from His royal coffers, we should have had cause to love Him eternally; but no, He will have His bride as rich as Himself, and He will not have a glory or a grace in which she shall not share. He has not been content with less than making us joint-heirs with Himself, so that we might have equal possessions. He has emptied all His estate into the coffers of the Church and hath all things common with His redeemed. There is not one room in His house the key of which He will withhold from His people. He gives them full liberty to take all that He hath to be their own; He loves them to make free with His treasure and appropriate as much as they can possibly carry. The boundless fulness of His all-sufficiency is as free to the believer as the air He breathes. Christ hath put the flagon of His love and grace to the believer's lip and bidden him drink on for ever; for could he drain it, he is welcome to do so, and as he cannot exhaust it, he is bidden to drink abundantly, for it is all his own. What truer proof of fellowship can heaven or earth afford?

> *When I stand before the throne*
> *Dressed in beauty not my own;*
> *When I see Thee as Thou art,*
> *Love Thee with unsinning heart;*
> *Then, Lord, shall I fully know—*
> *Not till then—how much I owe.*

Lead me in thy truth, and teach me:
for thou art the God of my salvation;
on thee do I wait all the day.
PSALM 25:5

When the believer has begun with trembling feet to walk in the way of the Lord, he asks to be still led onward like a little child upheld by its parent's helping hand, and he craves to be further instructed in the alphabet of truth. Experimental teaching is the burden of this prayer. David knew much, but he felt his ignorance and desired to be still in the Lord's school: Four times over in two verses he applies for a scholarship in the college of grace. It were well for many professors if instead of following their own devices and cutting out new paths of thought for themselves, they would enquire for the good old ways of God's own truth and beseech the Holy Ghost to give them sanctified understandings and teachable spirits. "For thou art the God of my salvation." The Three-One Jehovah is the Author and Perfecter of salvation to His people. Reader, is He the God of your salvation? Do you find in the Father's election, in the Son's atonement, and in the Spirit's quickening all the grounds of your eternal hopes? If so, you may use this as an argument for obtaining further blessings; if the Lord has ordained to save you, surely He will not refuse to instruct you in His ways. It is a happy thing when we can address the Lord with the confidence which David here manifests, it gives us great power in prayer and comfort in trial. "On thee do I wait all the day." Patience is the fair handmaid and daughter of faith; we cheerfully wait when we are certain that we shall not wait in vain. It is our duty and our privilege to wait upon the Lord in service, in worship, in expectancy, in trust all the days of our life. Our faith will be tried faith, and if it be of the true kind, it will bear continued trial without yielding. We shall not grow weary of waiting upon God if we remember how long and how graciously He once waited for us.

*When I cry unto thee,
then shall mine enemies turn back: this I know;
for God is for me.*
PSALM 56:9

It is impossible for any human speech to express the full meaning of this delightful phrase, "God is for me." He was "for us" before the worlds were made; He was "for us," or He would not have given His well-beloved Son; He was "for us" when He smote the only-begotten and laid the full weight of His wrath upon Him—He was "for us," though He was against Him; He was "for us," when we were ruined in the fall—he loved us notwithstanding all; He was "for us," when we were rebels against Him, and with a high hand were bidding Him defiance; He was "for us," or He would not have brought us humbly to seek His face. He has been "for us" in many struggles; we have been summoned to encounter hosts of dangers; we have been assailed by temptations from without and within—how could we have remained unharmed to this hour if He had not been "for us"? He is "for us" with all the infinity of His being; with all the omnipotence of His love; with all the infallibility of His wisdom; arrayed in all His divine attributes, He is "for us"—eternally and immutably "for us"; "for us" when yon blue skies shall be rolled up like a worn out vesture; "for us" throughout eternity. And because He is "for us," the voice of prayer will always ensure His help. "When I cry unto thee, then shall mine enemies be turned back." This is no uncertain hope, but a well grounded assurance—"this I know." I will direct my prayer unto thee and will look up for the answer, assured that it will come, and that mine enemies shall be defeated, "for God is for me." O believer, how happy art thou with the King of kings on thy side! How safe with such a Protector! How sure thy cause pleaded by such an Advocate! If God be for thee, who can be against thee?

The blood of Jesus Christ his Son cleanseth us from all sin.
1 JOHN 1:7

*C*leanseth," says the text—not "shall cleanse." There are multitudes who think that as a dying hope they may look forward to pardon. Oh! how infinitely better to have cleansing now than to depend on the bare possibility of forgiveness when I come to die. Some imagine that a sense of pardon is an attainment only obtainable after many years of Christian experience. But forgiveness of sin is a present thing—a privilege for this day, a joy for this very hour. The moment a sinner trusts Jesus he is fully forgiven. The text, being written in the present tense, also indicates continuance; it was "cleanseth" yesterday, it is "cleanseth" today, it will be "cleanseth" tomorrow: it will be always so with you, Christian, until you cross the river; every hour you may come to this fountain, for it cleanseth still. Notice, likewise, the completeness of the cleansing, "The blood of Jesus Christ His Son cleanseth us from all sin"—not only from sin, but "from all sin." Reader, I cannot tell you the exceeding sweetness of this word, but I pray God the Holy Ghost to give you a taste of it. Manifold are our sins against God. Whether the bill be little or great, the same receipt can discharge one as the other. The blood of Jesus Christ is as blessed and divine a payment for the transgressions of blaspheming Peter as for the shortcomings of loving John; our iniquity is gone, all gone at once, and all gone for ever. Blessed completeness! What a sweet theme to dwell upon as one gives himself to sleep.

> *Sins against a holy God;*
> *Sins against His righteous laws;*
> *Sins against His love, His blood;*
> *Sins against His name and cause;*
> *Sins immense as is the sea—*
> *From them all He cleanseth me.*

Who went about doing good.
ACTS 10:38

Few words, but yet an exquisite miniature of the Lord Jesus Christ. There are not many touches, but they are the strokes of a master's pencil. Of the Savior, and only of the Savior, is it true in the fullest, broadest, and most unqualified sense. "He went about doing good." From this description it is evident that He did good personally. The evangelists constantly tell us that He touched the leper with His own finger, that He anointed the eyes of the blind, and that in cases where He was asked to speak the word only at a distance, He did not usually comply, but went Himself to the sick bed and there personally wrought the cure. A lesson to us, if we would do good, to do it ourselves. Give alms with your own hand; a kind look or word will enhance the value of the gift. Speak to a friend about his soul; your loving appeal will have more influence than a whole library of tracts. Our Lord's mode of doing good sets forth His incessant activity! He did not only the good which came close to hand, but He "went about" on His errands of mercy. Throughout the whole land of Judea there was scarcely a village or a hamlet which was not gladdened by the sight of Him. How this reproves the creeping, loitering manner in which many professors serve the Lord. Let us gird up the loins of our mind and be not weary in well doing. Does not the text imply that Jesus Christ went out of His way to do good? "He went about doing good." He was never deterred by danger or difficulty. He sought out the objects of His gracious intentions. So must we. If old plans will not answer, we must try new ones, for fresh experiments sometimes achieve more than regular methods. Christ's perseverance and the unity of His purpose are also hinted at, and the practical application of the subject may be summed up in the words, "He hath left us an example that we should follow in His steps."

Him that cometh to me I will in no wise cast out.
JOHN 6:37

*N*o limit is set to the duration of this promise. It does not merely say, "I will not cast out a sinner at his first coming," but, "I will in no wise cast out." The original reads, "I will not, not cast out," or "I will never, never cast out." The text means, that Christ will not at first reject a believer; and that as He will not do it at first, so He will not to the last.

But suppose the believer sins after coming? "If any man sin we have an advocate with the Father, Jesus Christ the righteous." But suppose that believers backslide? "I will heal their backsliding, I will love them freely: for mine anger is turned away from him." But believers may fall under temptation! "God is faithful, who will not suffer you to be tempted above that ye are able; but will with the temptation also make a way to escape, that ye may be able to bear it." But the believer may fall into sin as David did! Yes, but He will "purge them with hyssop, and they shall be clean; he will wash them and they shall be whiter than snow"; "From all their iniquities will I cleanse them."

Once in Christ, in Christ for ever,
Nothing from His love can sever.

"I give unto my sheep," saith He, "eternal life; and they shall never perish, neither shall any man pluck them out of my hand." What sayest thou to this, O trembling feeble mind? Is not this a precious mercy, that coming to Christ, thou dost not come to One who will treat thee well for a little while, and then send thee about thy business, but He will receive thee and make thee His bride, and thou shalt be His for ever? Receive no longer the spirit of bondage again to fear, but the spirit of adoption whereby thou shalt cry, Abba, Father! Oh! the grace of these words: "I will in no wise cast out."

Thou crownest the year with thy goodness.
PSALM 65:11

All the year round, every hour of every day, God is richly blessing us; both when we sleep and when we wake, His mercy waits upon us. The sun may leave us a legacy of darkness, but our God never ceases to shine upon His children with beams of love. Like a river, His lovingkindness is always flowing, with a fulness inexhaustible as His own nature. Like the atmosphere which constantly surrounds the earth and is always ready to support the life of man, the benevolence of God surrounds all His creatures; in it, as in their element, they live and move and have their being. Yet as the sun on summer days gladdens us with beams more warm and bright than at other times, and as rivers are at certain seasons swollen by the rain, and as the atmosphere itself is sometimes fraught with more fresh, more bracing, or more balmy influences than heretofore, so is it with the mercy of God; it hath its golden hours; its days of overflow, when the Lord magnifieth His grace before the sons of men. Amongst the blessings of the nether springs, the joyous days of harvest are a special season of excessive favor. It is the glory of autumn that the ripe gifts of providence are then abundantly bestowed; it is the mellow season of realization, whereas all before was but hope and expectation. Great is the joy of harvest. Happy are the reapers who fill their arms with the liberality of heaven. The Psalmist tells us that the harvest is the crowning of the year. Surely these crowning mercies call for crowning thanksgiving! Let us render it by the inward emotions of gratitude. Let our hearts be warmed; let our spirits remember, meditate, and think upon this goodness of the Lord. Then let us praise Him with our lips and laud and magnify His name from whose bounty all this goodness flows. Let us glorify God by yielding our gifts to His cause. A practical proof of our gratitude is a special thank-offering to the Lord of the harvest.

Christ, who is our life.
COLOSSIANS 3:4

Paul's marvelously rich expression indicates that Christ is the source of our life. "You hath he quickened who were dead in trespasses and sins." That same voice which brought Lazarus out of the tomb raised us to newness of life. He is now the substance of our spiritual life. It is by His life that we live; He is in us, the hope of glory, the spring of our actions, the central thought which moves every other thought. Christ is the sustenance of our life. What can the Christian feed upon but Jesus' flesh and blood? "This is the bread which cometh down from heaven, that a man may eat thereof, and not die." O way-worn pilgrims in this wilderness of sin, you never get a morsel to satisfy the hunger of your spirits, except ye find it in Him! Christ is the solace of our life. All our true joys come from Him; and in times of trouble, His presence is our consolation. There is nothing worth living for but Him; and His lovingkindness is better than life! Christ is the object of our life. As speeds the ship towards the port, so hastes the believer towards the haven of his Savior's bosom. As flies the arrow to its goal, so flies the Christian towards the perfecting of his fellowship with Christ Jesus. As the soldier fights for his captain, and is crowned in his captain's victory, so the believer contends for Christ and gets his triumph out of the triumphs of his Master. "For him to live is Christ." Christ is the exemplar of our life. Where there is the same life within, there will, there must be, to a great extent, the same developments without; and if we live in near fellowship with the Lord Jesus we shall grow like Him. We shall set Him before us as our Divine copy, and we shall seek to tread in His footsteps, until He shall become the crown of our life in glory. Oh! how safe, how honored, how happy is the Christian, since Christ is our life!

The Son of man hath power on earth to forgive sins.
MATTHEW 9:6

*B*ehold one of the great Physician's mightiest arts: He has power to forgive sin! While here He lived below, before the ransom had been paid, before the blood had been literally sprinkled on the mercy-seat, He had power to forgive sin. Hath He not power to do it now that He hath died? What power must dwell in Him who to the utmost farthing has faithfully discharged the debts of His people! He has boundless power now that He has finished transgression and made an end of sin. If ye doubt it, see Him rising from the dead! behold Him in ascending splendor raised to the right hand of God! Hear Him pleading before the eternal Father, pointing to His wounds, urging the merit of His sacred passion! What power to forgive is here! "He hath ascended on high and received gifts for men." "He is exalted on high to give repentance and remission of sins." The most crimson sins are removed by the crimson of His blood. At this moment, dear reader, whatever thy sinfulness, Christ has power to pardon, power to pardon thee and millions such as thou art. A word will speak it. He has nothing more to do to win thy pardon; all the atoning work is done. He can, in answer to thy tears, forgive thy sins today and make thee know it. He can breathe into thy soul at this very moment a peace with God which passeth all understanding, which shall spring from perfect remission of thy manifold iniquities. Dost thou believe that? I trust thou believest it. Mayst thou experience now the power of Jesus to forgive sin! Waste no time in applying to the Physician of souls, but hasten to Him with words like these:—

Jesus! Master! hear my cry;
Save me, heal me with a word;
Fainting at Thy feet I lie,
Thou my whisper'd plaint hast heard.

And I will remember my covenant.
GENESIS 9:15

*M*ark the form of the promise. God does not say, "And when ye shall look upon the bow, and ye shall remember My covenant, then I will not destroy the earth," but it is gloriously put, not upon our memory, which is fickle and frail, but upon God's memory, which is infinite and immutable. "The bow shall be in the cloud; and I will look upon it, that I may remember the everlasting covenant." Oh! it is not my remembering God, it is God's remembering me which is the ground of my safety; it is not my laying hold of His covenant, but His covenant's laying hold on me. Glory be to God! the whole of the bulwarks of salvation are secured by divine power, and even the minor towers, which we may imagine might have been left to man, are guarded by almighty strength. Even the remembrance of the covenant is not left to our memories, for we might forget, but our Lord cannot forget the saints whom He has graven on the palms of His hands. It is with us as with Israel in Egypt; the blood was upon the lintel and the two sideposts, but the Lord did not say, "When you see the blood I will pass over you," but "When I see the blood I will pass over you." My looking to Jesus brings me joy and peace, but it is God's looking to Jesus which secures my salvation and that of all His elect, since it is impossible for our God to look at Christ, our bleeding Surety, and then to be angry with us for sins already punished in Him. No, it is not left with us even to be saved by remembering the covenant. There is no linsey-wolsey here—not a single thread of the creature mars the fabric. It is not of man, neither by man, but of the Lord alone. We should remember the covenant, and we shall do it, through divine grace; but the hinge of our safety does not hang there—it is God's remembering us, not our remembering Him; and hence the covenant is an everlasting covenant.

The mercy of God.
PSALM 52:8

*M*editate a little on this mercy of the Lord. It is tender mercy. With gentle, loving touch, He healeth the broken in heart and bindeth up their wounds. He is as gracious in the manner of His mercy as in the matter of it. It is great mercy. There is nothing little in God; His mercy is like Himself—it is infinite. You cannot measure it. His mercy is so great that it forgives great sins to great sinners, after great lengths of time, and then gives great favors and great privileges and raises us up to great enjoyments in the great heaven of the great God. It is undeserved mercy, as indeed all true mercy must be, for deserved mercy is only a misnomer for justice. There was no right on the sinner's part to the kind consideration of the Most High; had the rebel been doomed at once to eternal fire he would have richly merited the doom, and if delivered from wrath, sovereign love alone has found a cause, for there was none in the sinner himself. It is rich mercy. Some things are great, but have little efficacy in them, but this mercy is a cordial to your drooping spirits; a golden ointment to your bleeding wounds; a heavenly bandage to your broken bones; a royal chariot for your weary feet; a bosom of love for your trembling heart. It is manifold mercy. As Bunyan says, "All the flowers in God's garden are double." There is no single mercy. You may think you have but one mercy, but you shall find it to be a whole cluster of mercies. It is abounding mercy. Millions have received it, yet far from its being exhausted; it is as fresh, as full, and as free as ever. It is unfailing mercy. It will never leave Thee. If mercy be thy friend, mercy will be with thee in temptation to keep thee from yielding; with thee in trouble to prevent thee from sinking; with thee living to be the light and life of thy countenance; and with thee dying to be the joy of thy soul when earthly comfort is ebbing fast.

That Christ may dwell in your hearts by faith.
EPHESIANS 3:17

*B*eyond measure it is desirable that we, as believers, should have the person of Jesus constantly before us to inflame our love towards Him and to increase our knowledge of Him. I would to God that my readers were all entered as diligent scholars in Jesus' college, students of Corpus Christi, or the body of Christ, resolved to attain unto a good degree in the learning of the cross. But to have Jesus ever near, the heart must be full of Him, welling up with His love, even to overrunning; hence the apostle prays "that Christ may dwell in your hearts." See how near he would have Jesus to be! You cannot get a subject closer to you than to have it in the heart itself. "That he may dwell"; not that He may call upon you sometimes, as a casual visitor enters into a house and tarries for a night, but that He may dwell; that Jesus may become the Lord and Tenant of your inmost being, never more to go out.

Observe the words—that He may dwell in your heart, that best room of the house of manhood; not in your thoughts alone, but in your affections; not merely in the mind's meditations, but in the heart's emotions. We should pant after love to Christ of a most abiding character, not a love that flames up and then dies out into the darkness of a few embers, but a constant flame, fed by sacred fuel, like the fire upon the altar which never went out. This cannot be accomplished except by faith. Faith must be strong, or love will not be fervent; the root of the flower must be healthy, or we cannot expect the bloom to be sweet. Faith is the lily's root, and love is the lily's bloom. Now, reader, Jesus cannot be in your heart's love except you have a firm hold of Him by your heart's faith; and, therefore, pray that you may always trust Christ in order that you may always love Him. If love be cold, be sure that faith is drooping.

On mine arm shall they trust.
ISAIAH 51:5

In seasons of severe trial, the Christian has nothing on earth that he can trust to and is therefore compelled to cast himself on his God alone. When his vessel is on its beam-ends, and no human deliverance can avail, he must simply and entirely trust himself to the providence and care of God. Happy storm that wrecks a man on such a rock as this! O blessed hurricane that drives the soul to God and God alone! There is no getting at our God sometimes because of the multitude of our friends; but when a man is so poor, so friendless, so helpless that he has nowhere else to turn, he flies into his Father's arms and is blessedly clasped therein! When he is burdened with troubles so pressing and so peculiar, that he cannot tell them to any but his God, he may be thankful for them; for he will learn more of his Lord then than at any other time. Oh, tempest-tossed believer, it is a happy trouble that drives thee to thy Father! Now that thou hast only thy God to trust to, see that thou puttest thy full confidence in Him. Dishonor not thy Lord and Master by unworthy doubts and fears; but be strong in faith, giving glory to God. Show the world that thy God is worth ten thousand worlds to thee. Show rich men how rich thou art in thy poverty when the Lord God is thy helper. Show the strong man how strong thou art in thy weakness when underneath thee are the everlasting arms. Now is the time for feats of faith and valiant exploits. Be strong and very courageous, and the Lord thy God shall certainly, as surely as He built the heavens and the earth, glorify Himself in thy weakness and magnify His might in the midst of thy distress. The grandeur of the arch of heaven would be spoiled if the sky were supported by a single visible column, and your faith would lose its glory if it rested on anything discernible by the carnal eye. May the Holy Spirit give you to rest in Jesus this closing day of the month.

This man receiveth sinners.
LUKE 15:2

*O*bserve the condescension of this fact. This Man, who towers above all other men, holy, harmless, undefiled, and separate from sinners—this Man receiveth sinners. This Man, who is no other than the eternal God, before whom angels veil their faces—this Man receiveth sinners. It needs an angel's tongue to describe such a mighty stoop of love. That any of us should be willing to seek after the lost is nothing wonderful—they are of our own race; but that He, the offended God, against whom the transgression has been committed, should take upon Himself the form of a servant and bear the sin of many and should then be willing to receive the vilest of the vile, this is marvellous.

"This Man receiveth sinners"; not, however, that they may remain sinners, but He receives them that He may pardon their sins, justify their persons, cleanse their hearts by His purifying word, preserve their souls by the indwelling of the Holy Ghost, and enable them to serve Him, to show forth His praise and to have communion with Him. Into His heart's love He receives sinners, takes them from the dunghill, and wears them as jewels in His crown; plucks them as brands from the burning and preserves them as costly monuments of His mercy. None are so precious in Jesus' sight as the sinners for whom He died. When Jesus receives sinners, He has not some out-of-doors reception place, no casual ward where He charitably entertains them as men do passing beggars, but He opens the golden gates of His royal heart and receives the sinner right into Himself—yea, He admits the humble penitent into personal union and makes him a member of His body, of His flesh, and of His bones. There was never such a reception as this! This fact is still most sure this evening, He is still receiving sinners: Would to God sinners would receive Him.

The liberty wherewith Christ hath made us free.
GALATIANS 5:1

This "liberty" makes us free to heaven's charter—the Bible. Here is a choice passage, Believer, "When thou passest through the rivers, I will be with thee." You are free to that. Here is another: "The mountains shall depart, and the hills be removed; but my kindness shall not depart from thee"; you are free to that. You are a welcome guest at the table of the promises. Scripture is a never-failing treasury filled with boundless stores of grace. It is the bank of heaven; you may draw from it as much as you please, without let or hindrance. Come in faith and you are welcome to all covenant blessings. There is not a promise in the Word which shall be withheld. In the depths of tribulations let this freedom comfort you; amidst waves of distress let it cheer you; when sorrows surround thee let it be thy solace. This is thy Father's love-token; thou art free to it at all times. Thou art also free to the throne of grace. It is the believer's privilege to have access at all times to His heavenly Father. Whatever our desires, our difficulties, our wants, we are at liberty to spread all before Him. It matters not how much we may have sinned, we may ask and expect pardon. It signifies nothing how poor we are, we may plead His promise that He will provide all things needful. We have permission to approach His throne at all times—in midnight's darkest hour or in noontide's most burning heat. Exercise thy right, O believer, and live up to thy privilege. Thou art free to all that is treasured up in Christ—wisdom, righteousness, sanctification, and redemption. It matters not what thy need is, for there is fulness of supply in Christ, and it is there for thee. O what a "freedom" is thine! freedom from condemnation, freedom to the promises, freedom to the throne of grace, and at last freedom to enter heaven!

The LORD looketh from heaven;
he beholdeth all the sons of men.
PSALM 33:13

*P*erhaps no figure of speech represents God in a more gracious light than when He is spoken of as stooping from His throne and coming down from heaven to attend to the wants and to behold the woes of mankind. We love Him, who, when Sodom and Gomorrah were full of iniquity, would not destroy those cities until He had made a personal visitation of them. We cannot help pouring out our heart in affection for our Lord who inclines His ear from the highest glory and puts it to the lip of the dying sinner, whose failing heart longs after reconciliation. How can we but love Him when we know that He numbers the very hairs of our heads, marks our path, and orders our ways? Specially is this great truth brought near to our heart, when we recollect how attentive He is, not merely to the temporal interests of His creatures, but to their spiritual concerns. Though leagues of distance lie between the finite creature and the infinite Creator, yet there are links uniting both. When a tear is wept by thee, think not that God doth not behold; for, "Like as a father pitieth his children, so the Lord pitieth them that fear him." Thy sigh is able to move the heart of Jehovah; thy whisper can incline His ear unto thee; thy prayer can stay His hand; thy faith can move His arm. Think not that God sits on high taking no account of thee. Remember that however poor and needy thou art, yet the Lord thinketh upon thee. For the eyes of the Lord run to and fro throughout the whole earth, to show Himself strong in the behalf of them whose heart is perfect towards Him.

Oh! then repeat the truth that never tires;
No God is like the God my soul desires;
He at whose voice heaven trembles, even He,
Great as He is, knows how to stoop to me.

The LORD will give grace and glory.
PSALM 84:11

Bounteous is Jehovah in His nature; to give is His delight. His gifts are beyond measure precious and are as freely given as the light of the sun. He gives grace to His elect because He wills it, to His redeemed because of His covenant, to the called because of His promise, to believers because they seek it, to sinners because they need it. He gives grace abundantly, seasonably, constantly, readily, sovereignly; doubly enhancing the value of the boon by the manner of its bestowal. Grace in all its forms He freely renders to His people: Comforting, preserving, sanctifying, directing, instructing, assisting grace; He generously pours into their souls without ceasing; and He always will do so, whatever may occur. Sickness may befall, but the Lord will give grace; poverty may happen to us, but grace will surely be afforded; death must come, but grace will light a candle at the darkest hour. Reader, how blessed it is as years roll round, and the leaves begin again to fall, to enjoy such an unfading promise as this, "The Lord will give grace."

The little conjunction *and* in this verse is a diamond rivet binding the present with the future: Grace and glory always go together. God has married them, and none can divorce them. The Lord will never deny a soul glory to whom He has freely given to live upon His grace; indeed, glory is nothing more than grace in its Sabbath dress, grace in full bloom, grace like autumn fruit, mellow and perfected. How soon we may have glory none can tell! It may be before this month of October has run out we shall see the Holy City; but be the interval longer or shorter, we shall be glorified ere long. Glory, the glory of heaven, the glory of eternity, the glory of Jesus, the glory of the Father, the Lord will surely give to His chosen. Oh, rare promise of a faithful God!

Two golden links of one celestial chain:
Who owneth grace shall surely glory gain.

If any man sin, we have an advocate with the Father,
Jesus Christ the righteous.
1 JOHN 2:1

"If any man sin, we have an advocate." Yes, though we sin, we have Him still. John does not say, "If any man sin, he has forfeited his advocate," but "we have an advocate," sinners though we are. All the sin that a believer ever did, or can be allowed to commit, cannot destroy his interest in the Lord Jesus Christ as his advocate. The name here given to our Lord is suggestive. "Jesus." Ah! then He is an advocate such as we need, for Jesus is the name of one whose business and delight it is to save. "They shall call His name Jesus, for he shall save his people from their sins." His sweetest name implies His success. Next, it is "Jesus Christ"—Christos, the anointed. This shows His authority to plead. The Christ has a right to plead, for He is the Father's own appointed advocate and elected priest. If He were of our choosing He might fail, but if God hath laid help upon one that is mighty, we may safely lay our trouble where God has laid His help. He is Christ, and therefore authorized; He is Christ, and therefore qualified, for the anointing has fully fitted Him for His work. He can plead so as to move the heart of God and prevail. What words of tenderness, what sentences of persuasion will the anointed use when He stands up to plead for me! One more letter of His name remains, "Jesus Christ the righteous." This is not only His character but His plea. It is His character, and if the Righteous One be my advocate, then my cause is good, or He would not have espoused it. It is His plea, for He meets the charge of unrighteousness against me by the plea that He is righteous. He declares Himself my substitute and puts His obedience to my account. My soul, thou hast a friend well fitted to be thine advocate, He cannot but succeed; leave thyself entirely in His hands.

Whosoever drinketh of the water
that I shall give him shall never thirst.
JOHN 4:14

He who is a believer in Jesus finds enough in his Lord to satisfy him now and to content him forevermore. The believer is not the man whose days are weary for want of comfort and whose nights are long from absence of heart-cheering thought, for he finds in religion such a spring of joy, such a fountain of consolation, that he is content and happy. Put him in a dungeon, and he will find good company; place him in a barren wilderness, he will eat the bread of heaven; drive him away from friendship, he will meet the "friend that sticketh closer than a brother." Blast all his gourds, and he will find shadow beneath the Rock of Ages; sap the foundation of his earthly hopes, but his heart will still be fixed, trusting in the Lord. The heart is as insatiable as the grave till Jesus enters it, and then it is a cup full to overflowing. There is such a fulness in Christ that He alone is the believer's all. The true saint is so completely satisfied with the all-sufficiency of Jesus that He thirsts no more—except it be for deeper draughts of the living fountain. In that sweet manner, Believer, shalt thou thirst; it shall not be a thirst of pain, but of loving desire; thou wilt find it a sweet thing to be panting after a fuller enjoyment of Jesus' love. One in days of yore said, "I have been sinking my bucket down into the well full often, but now my thirst after Jesus has become so insatiable, that I long to put the well itself to my lips and drink right on." Is this the feeling of thine heart now, Believer? Dost thou feel that all thy desires are satisfied in Jesus, and that thou hast no want now but to know more of Him and to have closer fellowship with Him? Then come continually to the fountain and take of the water of life freely. Jesus will never think you take too much but will ever welcome you, saying, "Drink, yea, drink abundantly, O beloved."

And I will deliver thee out of the hand of the wicked,
and I will redeem thee out of the hand of the terrible.
JEREMIAH 15:21

Note the glorious personality of the promise. I will, I will. The Lord Jehovah Himself interposes to deliver and redeem His people. He pledges Himself personally to rescue them. His own arm shall do it, that He may have the glory. Here is not a word said of any effort of our own which may be needed to assist the Lord. Neither our strength nor our weakness is taken into the account, but the lone I, like the sun in the heavens, shines out resplendent in all-sufficience. Why then do we calculate our forces and consult with flesh and blood to our grievous wounding? Jehovah has power enough without borrowing from our puny arm. Peace, ye unbelieving thoughts, be still, and know that the Lord reigneth. Nor is there a hint concerning secondary means and causes. The Lord says nothing of friends and helpers: He undertakes the work alone and feels no need of human arms to aid Him. Vain are all our lookings around to companions and relatives; they are broken reeds if we lean upon them—often unwilling when able, and unable when they are willing. Since the promise comes alone from God, it would be well to wait only upon Him; and when we do so, our expectation never fails us. Who are the wicked that we should fear them? The Lord will utterly consume them; they are to be pitied rather than feared. As for terrible ones, they are only terrors to those who have no God to fly to, for when the Lord is on our side, whom shall we fear? If we run into sin to please the wicked, we have cause to be alarmed, but if we hold fast our integrity, the rage of tyrants shall be overruled for our good. When the fish swallowed Jonah, he found him a morsel which he could not digest; and when the world devours the church, it is glad to be rid of it again. In all times of fiery trial, in patience let us possess our souls.

Jesus saith unto them, Come and dine.
JOHN 21:12

In these words the believer is invited to a holy nearness to Jesus. "Come and dine" implies the same table, the same meat; ay, and sometimes it means to sit side by side and lean our head upon the Savior's bosom. It is being brought into the banqueting-house, where waves the banner of redeeming love. "Come and dine" gives us a vision of union with Jesus, because the only food that we can feast upon when we dine with Jesus is Himself. Oh, what union is this! It is a depth which reason cannot fathom, that we thus feed upon Jesus. "He that eateth my flesh, and drinketh my blood, dwelleth in me, and I in Him." It is also an invitation to enjoy fellowship with the saints. Christians may differ on a variety of points, but they have all one spiritual appetite; and if we cannot all feel alike, we can all feed alike on the bread of life sent down from heaven. At the table of fellowship with Jesus we are one bread and one cup. As the loving cup goes round we pledge one another heartily therein. Get nearer to Jesus, and you will find yourself linked more and more in spirit to all who are like yourself, supported by the same heavenly manna. If we were more near to Jesus we should be more near to one another. We likewise see in these words the source of strength for every Christian. To look at Christ is to live, but for strength to serve Him you must "come and dine." We labor under much unnecessary weakness on account of neglecting this precept of the Master. We none of us need to put ourselves on low diet; on the contrary, we should fatten on the marrow and fatness of the gospel that we may accumulate strength therein and urge every power to its full tension in the Master's service. Thus, then, if you would realize nearness to Jesus, union with Jesus, love to His people, and strength from Jesus, "come and dine" with Him by faith.

He shall gather the lambs with his arm.
ISAIAH 40:11

*O*ur good Shepherd has in His flock a variety of experiences, some are strong in the Lord, and others are weak in faith, but He is impartial in His care for all His sheep, and the weakest lamb is as dear to Him as the most advanced of the flock. Lambs are wont to lag behind, prone to wander, and apt to grow weary, but from all the danger of these infirmities the Shepherd protects them with His arm of power. He finds newborn souls, like young lambs, ready to perish—He nourishes them till life becomes vigorous; He finds weak minds ready to faint and die—He consoles them and renews their strength. All the little ones He gathers, for it is not the will of our heavenly Father that one of them should perish. What a quick eye He must have to see them all! What a tender heart to care for them all! What a far-reaching and potent arm, to gather them all! In His lifetime on earth He was a great gatherer of the weaker sort, and now that He dwells in heaven, His loving heart yearns towards the meek and contrite, the timid and feeble, the fearful and fainting here below. How gently did He gather me to Himself, to His truth, to His blood, to His love, to His church! With what effectual grace did He compel me to come to Himself! Since my first conversion, how frequently has He restored me from my wanderings and once again folded me within the circle of His everlasting arm! The best of all is, that He does it all Himself personally, not delegating the task of love, but condescending Himself to rescue and preserve His most unworthy servant. How shall I love Him enough or serve Him worthily? I would fain make His name great unto the ends of the earth, but what can my feebleness do for him? Great Shepherd, add to Thy mercies this one other, a heart to love Thee more truly as I ought.

The love of Christ constraineth us.
2 Corinthians 5:14

How much owest thou unto my Lord? Has He ever done anything for thee? Has He forgiven thy sins? Has He covered thee with a robe of righteousness? Has He set thy feet upon a rock? Has He established thy goings? Has He prepared heaven for thee? Has He prepared thee for heaven? Has He written thy name in His book of life? Has He given thee countless blessings? Has He laid up for thee a store of mercies, which eye hath not seen nor ear heard? Then do something for Jesus worthy of His love. Give not a mere wordy offering to a dying Redeemer. How will you feel when your Master comes, if you have to confess that you did nothing for Him, but kept your love shut up, like a stagnant pool, neither flowing forth to His poor or to His work. Out on such love as that! What do men think of a love which never shows itself in action? Why, they say, "Open rebuke is better than secret love." Who will accept a love so weak that it does not actuate you to a single deed of self-denial, of generosity, of heroism, or zeal! Think how He has loved you and given Himself for you! Do you know the power of that love? Then let it be like a rushing mighty wind to your soul to sweep out the clouds of your worldliness and clear away the mists of sin. "For Christ's sake" be this the tongue of fire that shall sit upon you: "For Christ's sake" be this the divine rapture, the heavenly afflatus to bear you aloft from earth, the divine spirit that shall make you bold as lions and swift as eagles in your Lord's service. Love should give wings to the feet of service and strength to the arms of labor. Fixed on God with a constancy that is not to be shaken, resolute to honor Him with a determination that is not to be turned aside, and pressing on with an ardour never to be wearied, let us manifest the constraints of love to Jesus. May the divine loadstone draw us heavenward towards itself!

I will love them freely.
HOSEA 14:4

*T*his sentence is a body of divinity in miniature. He who understands its meaning is a theologian, and he who can dive into its fulness is a true master in Israel. It is a condensation of the glorious message of salvation which was delivered to us in Christ Jesus our Redeemer. The sense hinges upon the word "freely." This is the glorious, the suitable, the divine way by which love streams from heaven to earth, a spontaneous love flowing forth to those who neither deserved it, purchased it, nor sought after it. It is, indeed, the only way in which God can love such as we are. The text is a death-blow to all sorts of fitness: "I will love them freely." Now, if there were any fitness necessary in us, then He would not love us freely, at least, this would be a mitigation and a drawback to the freeness of it. But it stands, "I will love you freely." We complain, "Lord, my heart is so hard." "I will love you freely." "But I do not feel my need of Christ as I could wish." "I will not love you because you feel your need; I will love you freely." "But I do not feel that softening of spirit which I could desire." Remember, the softening of spirit is not a condition, for there are no conditions; the covenant of grace has no conditionality whatever; so that we without any fitness may venture upon the promise of God which was made to us in Christ Jesus, when He said, "He that believeth on him is not condemned." It is blessed to know that the grace of God is free to us at all times, without preparation, without fitness, without money, and without price! "I will love them freely." These words invite backsliders to return: Indeed, the text was specially written for such—"I will heal their backsliding, I will love them freely." Backslider! surely the generosity of the promise will at once break your heart, and you will return and seek your injured Father's face.

I am the LORD, I change not.
MALACHI 3:6

*O*t is well for us that, amidst all the variableness of life, there is One whom change cannot affect, One whose heart can never alter, and on whose brow mutability can make no furrows. All things else have changed—all things are changing. The sun itself grows dim with age; the world is waxing old; the folding up of the worn-out vesture has commenced; the heavens and earth must soon pass away; they shall perish, they shall wax old as doth a garment; but there is One who only hath immortality, of whose years there is no end, and in whose person there is no change. The delight which the mariner feels, when, after having been tossed about for many a day, he steps again upon the solid shore, is the satisfaction of a Christian when, amidst all the changes of this troublous life, he rests the foot of his faith upon this truth—"I am the LORD, I change not."

The stability which the anchor gives the ship when it has at last obtained a hold-fast, is like that which the Christian's hope affords him when it fixes itself upon this glorious truth. With God "is no variableness, neither shadow of turning." Whatever His attributes were of old, they are now; His power, His wisdom, His justice, His truth, are alike unchanged. He has ever been the refuge of His people, their stronghold in the day of trouble, and He is their sure Helper still. He is unchanged in His love. He has loved His people with "an everlasting love"; He loves them now as much as ever He did, and when all earthly things shall have melted in the last conflagration, His love will still wear the dew of its youth. Precious is the assurance that He changes not! The wheel of providence revolves, but its axle is eternal love.

Death and change are busy ever,
Man decays, and ages move;
But His mercy waneth never;
God is wisdom, God is love.

In thy light shall we see light.
PSALM 36:9

No lips can tell the love of Christ to the heart till Jesus Himself shall speak within. Descriptions all fall flat and tame unless the Holy Ghost fills them with life and power; till our Immanuel reveals Himself within, the soul sees Him not. If you would see the sun, would you gather together the common means of illumination and seek in that way to behold the orb of day? No, the wise man knoweth that the sun must reveal itself, and only by its own blaze can that mighty lamp be seen. It is so with Christ. "Blessed art thou, Simon Barjona," said He to Peter, "for flesh and blood hath not revealed this unto thee." Purify flesh and blood by any educational process you may select, elevate mental faculties to the highest degree of intellectual power, yet none of these can reveal Christ. The Spirit of God must come with power and overshadow the man with his wings, and then in that mystic holy of holies the Lord Jesus must display Himself to the sanctified eye, as He doth not unto the purblind sons of men. Christ must be His own mirror. The great mass of this blear-eyed world can see nothing of the ineffable glories of Immanuel. He stands before them without form or comeliness, a root out of a dry ground, rejected by the vain and despised by the proud. Only where the Spirit has touched the eye with eye-salve, quickened the heart with divine life, and educated the soul to a heavenly taste, only there is He understood. "To you that believe he is precious"; to you He is the chief cornerstone, the Rock of your salvation, your all in all; but to others He is "a stone of stumbling and a rock of offence." Happy are those to whom our Lord manifests Himself, for His promise to such is that He will make His abode with them. O Jesus, our Lord, our heart is open, come in and go out no more forever. Show Thyself to us now! Favor us with a glimpse of Thine all-conquering charms.

The eternal God is thy refuge.
DEUTERONOMY 33:27

The word refuge may be translated "mansion" or "abiding-place," which gives the thought that God is our abode, our home. There is a fulness and sweetness in the metaphor, for dear to our hearts is our home, although it be the humblest cottage or the scantiest garret; and dearer far is our blessed God, in whom we live and move and have our being. It is at home that we feel safe: We shut the world out and dwell in quiet security. So when we are with our God we "fear no evil." He is our shelter and retreat, our abiding refuge. At home we take our rest; it is there we find repose after the fatigue and toil of the day. And so our hearts find rest in God, when, wearied with life's conflict, we turn to Him, and our soul dwells at ease. At home, also, we let our hearts loose; we are not afraid of being misunderstood, nor of our words being misconstrued. So when we are with God we can commune freely with Him, laying open all our hidden desires; for if the "secret of the Lord is with them that fear him," the secrets of them that fear Him ought to be, and must be, with their Lord. Home, too, is the place of our truest and purest happiness, and it is in God that our hearts find their deepest delight. We have joy in Him which far surpasses all other joy. It is also for home that we work and labor. The thought of it gives strength to bear the daily burden and quickens the fingers to perform the task; and in this sense we may also say that God is our home. Love to Him strengthens us. We think of Him in the person of His dear Son; and a glimpse of the suffering face of the Redeemer constrains us to labor in His cause. We feel that we must work, for we have brethren yet to be saved, and we have our Father's heart to make glad by bringing home His wandering sons; we would fill with holy mirth the sacred family among whom we dwell. Happy are those who have thus the God of Jacob for their refuge!

Underneath are the everlasting arms.
DEUTERONOMY 33:27

God—the eternal God—is Himself our support at all times, and especially when we are sinking in deep trouble. There are seasons when the Christian sinks very low in humiliation. Under a deep sense of his great sinfulness, he is humbled before God till he scarcely knows how to pray, because he appears, in his own sight, so worthless. Well, child of God, remember that when thou art at thy worst and lowest, yet "underneath" thee "are the everlasting arms." Sin may drag thee ever so low, but Christ's great atonement is still under all. You may have descended into the deeps, but you cannot have fallen so low as "the uttermost"; and to the uttermost He saves. Again, the Christian sometimes sinks very deeply in sore trial from without. Every earthly prop is cut away. What then? Still underneath him are "the everlasting arms." He cannot fall so deep in distress and affliction but what the covenant grace of an ever-faithful God will still encircle him. The Christian may be sinking under trouble from within through fierce conflict, but even then he cannot be brought so low as to be beyond the reach of the "everlasting arms"—they are underneath him; and, while thus sustained, all Satan's efforts to harm him avail nothing.

This assurance of support is a comfort to any weary but earnest worker in the service of God. It implies a promise of strength for each day, grace for each need, and power for each duty. And, further, when death comes, the promise shall still hold good. When we stand in the midst of Jordan, we shall be able to say with David, "I will fear no evil, for thou art with me." We shall descend into the grave, but we shall go no lower, for the eternal arms prevent our further fall. All through life, and at its close, we shall be upheld by the "everlasting arms"— arms that neither flag nor lose their strength, for "the everlasting God fainteth not, neither is weary."

And it came to pass in those days,
that he went out into a mountain to pray,
and continued all night in prayer to God.
LUKE 6:12

If ever one of woman born might have lived without prayer, it was our spotless, perfect Lord, and yet none was ever so much in supplication as He! Such was His love to His Father, that He loved much to be in communion with Him: such His love for His people, that He desired to be much in intercession for them. The fact of this eminent prayerfulness of Jesus is a lesson for us—He hath given us an example that we may follow in His steps. The time He chose was admirable, it was the hour of silence, when the crowd would not disturb Him; the time of inaction, when all but Himself had ceased to labor; and the season when slumber made men forget their woes and cease their applications to Him for relief. While others found rest in sleep, He refreshed himself with prayer. The place was also well selected. He was alone where none would intrude, where none could observe: Thus was He free from Pharisaic ostentation and vulgar interruption. Those dark and silent hills were a fit oratory for the Son of God. Heaven and earth in midnight stillness heard the groans and sighs of the mysterious Being in whom both worlds were blended. The continuance of His pleadings is remarkable; the long watches were not too long; the cold wind did not chill His devotions; the grim darkness did not darken His faith, or loneliness check His importunity. We cannot watch with Him one hour, but He watched for us whole nights. The occasion for this prayer is notable; it was after His enemies had been enraged—prayer was His refuge and solace; it was before He sent forth the twelve apostles—prayer was the gate of His enterprise, the herald of His new work. Should we not learn from Jesus to resort to special prayer when we are under peculiar trial, or contemplate fresh endeavors for the Master's glory? Lord Jesus, teach us to pray.

The LORD's portion is his people.
DEUTERONOMY 32:9

How are they His? By His own sovereign choice. He chose them and set His love upon them. This He did altogether apart from any goodness in them at the time, or any goodness which He foresaw in them. He had mercy on whom He would have mercy and ordained a chosen company unto eternal life; thus, therefore, are they His by His unconstrained election.

They are not only His by choice, but by purchase. He has bought and paid for them to the utmost farthing, hence about His title there can be no dispute. Not with corruptible things, as with silver and gold, but with the precious blood of the Lord Jesus Christ, the Lord's portion has been fully redeemed. There is no mortgage on His estate; no suits can be raised by opposing claimants, the price was paid in open court, and the Church is the Lord's freehold for ever. See the blood-mark upon all the chosen, invisible to human eye, but known to Christ, for "the Lord knoweth them that are his"; He forgetteth none of those whom He has redeemed from among men; He counts the sheep for whom He laid down His life and remembers well the Church for which He gave Himself.

They are also His by conquest. What a battle He had in us before we would be won! How long He laid siege to our hearts! how often He sent us terms of capitulation! but we barred our gates and fenced our walls against Him. Do we not remember that glorious hour when He carried our hearts by storm? when He placed His cross against the wall and scaled our ramparts, planting on our strongholds the blood-red flag of His omnipotent mercy? Yes, we are, indeed, the conquered captives of His omnipotent love. Thus chosen, purchased, and subdued, the rights of our divine possessor are inalienable: we rejoice that we never can be our own; and we desire, day by day, to do His will and to show forth His glory.

*O*bserve how positively the prophet speaks. He doth not say, "I hope, I trust, I sometimes think, that God hath pleaded the causes of my soul"; but he speaks of it as a matter of fact not to be disputed. "Thou hast pleaded the causes of my soul." Let us, by the aid of the gracious Comforter, shake off those doubts and fears which so much mar our peace and comfort. Be this our prayer, that we may have done with the harsh croaking voice of surmise and suspicion, and may be able to speak with the clear, melodious voice of full assurance. Notice how gratefully the prophet speaks, ascribing all the glory to God alone! You perceive there is not a word concerning himself or his own pleadings. He doth not ascribe his deliverance in any measure to any man, much less to his own merit; but it is "thou"—"O Lord, thou hast pleaded the causes of my soul; thou hast redeemed my life." A grateful spirit should ever be cultivated by the Christian; and especially after deliverances we should prepare a song for our God. Earth should be a temple filled with the songs of grateful saints, and every day should be a censer smoking with the sweet incense of thanksgiving. How joyful Jeremiah seems to be while he records the Lord's mercy. How triumphantly he lifts up the strain! He has been in the low dungeon and is even now no other than the weeping prophet; and yet in the very book which is called "Lamentations," clear as the song of Miriam when she dashed her fingers against the tabor, shrill as the note of Deborah when she met Barak with shouts of victory, we hear the voice of Jeremy going up to heaven—"Thou hast pleaded the causes of my soul; thou hast redeemed my life." O children of God, seek after a vital experience of the Lord's lovingkindness, and when you have it, speak positively of it; sing gratefully; shout triumphantly.

The forgiveness of sins, according to the riches of his grace.
EPHESIANS 1:7

*C*an there be a sweeter word in any language than that word "forgiveness" when it sounds in a guilty sinner's ear, like the silver notes of jubilee to the captive Israelite? Blessed, for ever blessed be that dear star of pardon which shines into the condemned cell and gives the perishing a gleam of hope amid the midnight of despair! Can it be possible that sin, such sin as mine, can be forgiven, forgiven altogether and forever? Hell is my portion as a sinner—there is no possibility of my escaping from it while sin remains upon me—can the load of guilt be uplifted, the crimson stain removed? Can the adamantine stones of my prison-house ever be loosed from their mortices, or the doors be lifted from their hinges? Jesus tells me that I may yet be clear. Forever blessed be the revelation of atoning love which not only tells me that pardon is possible, but that it is secured to all who rest in Jesus. I have believed in the appointed propitiation, even Jesus crucified, and therefore my sins are at this moment and forever, forgiven by virtue of His substitutionary pains and death. What joy is this! What bliss to be a perfectly pardoned soul! My soul dedicates all her powers to Him who of His own unpurchased love became my surety, and wrought out for me redemption through His blood. What riches of grace does free forgiveness exhibit! To forgive at all, to forgive fully, to forgive freely, to forgive forever! Here is a constellation of wonders; and when I think of how great my sins were, how dear were the precious drops which cleansed me from them, and how gracious was the method by which pardon was sealed home to me, I am in a maze of wondering worshipping affection. I bow before the throne which absolves me, I clasp the cross which delivers me, I serve henceforth all my days the Incarnate God, through whom I am this night a pardoned soul.

Oh that men would praise the LORD for his goodness,
and for his wonderful works to the children of men.
PSALM 107:8

If we complained less and praised more, we should be happier, and God would be more glorified. Let us daily praise God for common mercies—common as we frequently call them, and yet so priceless, that when deprived of them we are ready to perish. Let us bless God for the eyes with which we behold the sun, for the health and strength to walk abroad, for the bread we eat, for the raiment we wear. Let us praise Him that we are not cast out among the hopeless, or confined amongst the guilty; let us thank Him for liberty, for friends, for family associations and comforts; let us praise Him, in fact, for everything which we receive from His bounteous hand, for we deserve little and yet are most plenteously endowed. But, Beloved, the sweetest and the loudest note in our songs of praise should be of redeeming love. God's redeeming acts towards His chosen are forever the favorite themes of their praise. If we know what redemption means, let us not withhold our sonnets of thanksgiving. We have been redeemed from the power of our corruptions, uplifted from the depth of sin in which we were naturally plunged. We have been led to the cross of Christ—our shackles of guilt have been broken off; we are no longer slaves, but children of the living God, and can antedate the period when we shall be presented before the throne without spot or wrinkle or any such thing. Even now by faith we wave the palm branch and wrap ourselves about with the fair linen which is to be our everlasting array, and shall we not unceasingly give thanks to the Lord our Redeemer? Child of God, canst thou be silent? Awake, awake, ye heritors of glory, and lead your captivity captive, as ye cry with David, "Bless the LORD, O my soul: and all that is within me, bless his holy name." Let the new month begin with new songs.

Ask, and it shall be given you.
MATTHEW 7:7

*W*e know of a place in England still existing, where a dole of bread is served to every passerby who chooses to ask for it. Whoever the traveler may be, he has but to knock at the door of St. Cross Hospital, and there is the dole of bread for him. Jesus Christ so loveth sinners that He has built a St. Cross Hospital, so that whenever a sinner is hungry, he has but to knock and have his wants supplied. Nay, He has done better; He has attached to this Hospital of the Cross a bath; and whenever a soul is black and filthy, it has but to go there and be washed. The fountain is always full, always efficacious. No sinner ever went into it and found that it could not wash away his stains. Sins which were scarlet and crimson have all disappeared, and the sinner has been whiter than snow. As if this were not enough, there is attached to this Hospital of the Cross a wardrobe, and a sinner making application simply as a sinner, may be clothed from head to foot; and if he wishes to be a soldier, he may not merely have a garment for ordinary wear, but armor which shall cover him from the sole of his foot to the crown of his head. If he asks for a sword, he shall have that given to him, and a shield, too. Nothing that is good for him shall be denied him. He shall have spending-money so long as he lives, and he shall have an eternal heritage of glorious treasure when he enters into the joy of his Lord.

If all these things are to be had by merely knocking at mercy's door, O my soul, knock hard this morning and ask large things of thy generous Lord. Leave not the throne of grace till all thy wants have been spread before the Lord and until by faith thou hast a comfortable prospect that they shall be all supplied. No bashfulness need retard when Jesus invites. No unbelief should hinder when Jesus promises. No cold-heartedness should restrain when such blessings are to be obtained.

Thou, O God, hast prepared of thy goodness for the poor.
PSALM 68:10

*A*ll God's gifts are prepared gifts laid up in store for wants foreseen. He anticipates our needs; and out of the fulness which He has treasured up in Christ Jesus, He provides of His goodness for the poor. You may trust Him for all the necessities that can occur, for He has infallibly foreknown every one of them. He can say of us in all conditions, "I knew that thou wouldst be this and that." A man goes a journey across the desert, and when he has made a day's advance and pitched his tent, he discovers that he wants many comforts and necessaries which he has not brought in his baggage. "Ah!" says he, "I did not foresee this: If I had this journey to go again, I should bring these things with me so necessary to my comfort." But God has marked with prescient eye all the requirements of his poor wandering children, and when those needs occur, supplies are ready. It is goodness which He has prepared for the poor in heart, goodness and goodness only. "My grace is sufficient for thee." "As thy days, so shall thy strength be."

Reader, is your heart heavy this evening? God knew it would be; the comfort which your heart wants is treasured in the sweet assurance of the text. You are poor and needy, but He has thought upon you and has the exact blessing which you require in store for you. Plead the promise, believe it, and obtain its fulfilment. Do you feel that you never were so consciously vile as you are now? Behold, the crimson fountain is open still, with all its former efficacy, to wash your sin away. Never shall you come into such a position that Christ cannot aid you. No pinch shall ever arrive in your spiritual affairs in which Jesus Christ shall not be equal to the emergency, for your history has all been foreknown and provided for in Jesus.

Therefore will the LORD wait, that
he may be gracious unto you.
ISAIAH 30:18

God often delays in answering prayer. We have several instances of this in sacred Scripture. Jacob did not get the blessing from the angel until near the dawn of day—he had to wrestle all night for it. The poor woman of Syrophenicia was answered not a word for a long while. Paul besought the Lord thrice that "the thorn in the flesh" might be taken from him, and he received no assurance that it should be taken away, but instead thereof, a promise that God's grace should be sufficient for him. If thou hast been knocking at the gate of mercy and hast received no answer, shall I tell thee why the mighty Maker hath not opened the door and let thee in? Our Father has reasons peculiar to Himself for thus keeping us waiting. Sometimes it is to show His power and His sovereignty, that men may know that Jehovah has a right to give or to withhold. More frequently the delay is for our profit. Thou art perhaps kept waiting in order that thy desires may be more fervent. God knows that delay will quicken and increase desire, and that if He keeps thee waiting thou wilt see thy necessity more clearly and wilt seek more earnestly, and that thou wilt prize the mercy all the more for its long tarrying. There may also be something wrong in thee which has need to be removed, before the joy of the Lord is given. Perhaps thy views of the Gospel plan are confused, or thou mayest be placing some little reliance on thyself, instead of trusting simply and entirely to the Lord Jesus. Or, God makes thee tarry awhile that He may the more fully display the riches of His grace to thee at last. Thy prayers are all filed in heaven, and if not immediately answered they are certainly not forgotten, but in a little while shall be fulfilled to thy delight and satisfaction. Let not despair make thee silent, but continue instant in earnest supplication.

My people shall dwell in quiet resting places.
Isaiah 32:18

Peace and rest belong not to the unregenerate, they are the peculiar possession of the Lord's people, and of them only. The God of Peace gives perfect peace to those whose hearts are stayed upon Him. When man was unfallen, his God gave him the flowery bowers of Eden as his quiet resting places; alas! how soon sin blighted the fair abode of innocence. In the day of universal wrath when the flood swept away a guilty race, the chosen family were quietly secured in the resting-place of the ark, which floated them from the old condemned world into the new earth of the rainbow and the covenant, herein typifying Jesus, the ark of our salvation. Israel rested safely beneath the blood-besprinkled habitations of Egypt when the destroying angel smote the first-born; and in the wilderness the shadow of the pillar of cloud and the flowing rock gave the weary pilgrims sweet repose. At this hour we rest in the promises of our faithful God, knowing that His words are full of truth and power; we rest in the doctrines of His word, which are consolation itself; we rest in the covenant of His grace, which is a haven of delight. More highly favored are we than David in Adullam or Jonah beneath his gourd, for none can invade or destroy our shelter. The person of Jesus is the quiet resting-place of His people, and when we draw near to Him in the breaking of the bread, in the hearing of the word, the searching of the Scriptures, prayer, or praise, we find any form of approach to Him to be the return of peace to our spirits.

> *I hear the words of love, I gaze upon the blood,*
> *I see the mighty sacrifice, and I have peace with God.*
> *'Tis everlasting peace, sure as Jehovah's name,*
> *'Tis stable as His steadfast throne, for evermore the same:*
> *The clouds may go and come, and storms may sweep my sky,*
> *This blood-sealed friendship changes not, the cross is ever*
> *nigh.*

Faithful is he that calleth you, who also will do it.
1 THESSALONIANS 5:24

*H*eaven is a place where we shall never sin; where we shall cease our constant watch against an indefatigable enemy, because there will be no tempter to ensnare our feet. There the wicked cease from troubling, and the weary are at rest. Heaven is the "undefiled inheritance"; it is the land of perfect holiness, and therefore of complete security. But do not the saints even on earth sometimes taste the joys of blissful security? The doctrine of God's word is, that all who are in union with the Lamb are safe; that all the righteous shall hold on their way; that those who have committed their souls to the keeping of Christ shall find Him a faithful and immutable preserver. Sustained by such a doctrine we can enjoy security even on earth; not that high and glorious security which renders us free from every slip, but that holy security which arises from the sure promise of Jesus that none who believe in Him shall ever perish, but shall be with Him where He is. Believer, let us often reflect with joy on the doctrine of the perseverance of the saints and honor the faithfulness of our God by a holy confidence in Him.

May our God bring home to you a sense of your safety in Christ Jesus! May He assure you that your name is graven on His hand and whisper in your ear the promise, "Fear not, I am with thee." Look upon Him, the great Surety of the covenant, as faithful and true, and, therefore, bound and engaged to present you, the weakest of the family, with all the chosen race, before the throne of God; and in such a sweet contemplation you will drink the juice of the spiced wine of the Lord's pomegranate and taste the dainty fruits of Paradise. You will have an antepast of the enjoyments which ravish the souls of the perfect saints above, if you can believe with unstaggering faith that "faithful is he that calleth you, who also will do it."

Come unto me.
MATTHEW 11:28

*T*he cry of the Christian religion is the gentle word, "Come." The Jewish law harshly said, "Go, take heed unto thy steps as to the path in which thou shalt walk. Break the commandments, and thou shalt perish; keep them, and thou shalt live." The law was a dispensation of terror, which drove men before it as with a scourge; the gospel draws with bands of love. Jesus is the good Shepherd going before His sheep, bidding them follow Him and ever leading them onwards with the sweet word, "Come." The law repels, the gospel attracts. The law shows the distance which there is between God and man; the gospel bridges that awful chasm and brings the sinner across it.

From the first moment of your spiritual life until you are ushered into glory, the language of Christ to you will be, "Come, come unto me." As a mother puts out her finger to her little child and woos it to walk by saying, "Come," even so does Jesus. He will always be ahead of you, bidding you follow Him as the soldier follows his captain. He will always go before you to pave your way and clear your path, and you shall hear His animating voice calling you after Him all through life; while in the solemn hour of death, His sweet words with which He shall usher you into the heavenly world shall be— "Come, ye blessed of my Father."

Nay, further, this is not only Christ's cry to you, but, if you be a believer, this is your cry to Christ— "Come! come!" You will be longing for His second advent; you will be saying, "Come quickly, even so come Lord Jesus." You will be panting for nearer and closer communion with Him. As His voice to you is "Come," your response to Him will be. "Come, Lord, and abide with me. Come and occupy alone the throne of my heart; reign there without a rival, and consecrate me entirely to Thy service."

I am the door: by me if any man enter in, he shall be saved,
and shall go in and out, and find pasture.
JOHN 10:9

Jesus, the great I AM, is the entrance into the true church, and the way of access to God Himself. He gives to the man who comes to God by Him four choice privileges.

1. He shall be saved. The fugitive manslayer passed the gate of the city of refuge, and was safe. Noah entered the door of the ark and was secure. None can be lost who take Jesus as the door of faith to their souls. Entrance through Jesus into peace is the guarantee of entrance by the same door into heaven. Jesus is the only door, an open door, a wide door, a safe door; and blessed is he who rests all his hope of admission to glory upon the crucified Redeemer.

2. He shall go in. He shall be privileged to go in among the divine family, sharing the children's bread, and participating in all their honors and enjoyments. He shall go in to the chambers of communion, to the banquets of love, to the treasures of the covenant, to the storehouses of the promises. He shall go in unto the King of kings in the power of the Holy Spirit, and the secret of the Lord shall be with him.

3. He shall go out. This blessing is much forgotten. We go out into the world to labor and suffer, but what a mercy to go in the name and power of Jesus! We are called to bear witness to the truth, to cheer the disconsolate, to warn the careless, to win souls, and to glorify God; and as the angel said to Gideon, "Go in this thy might," even thus the Lord would have us proceed as His messengers in His name and strength.

4. He shall find pasture. He who knows Jesus shall never want. Going in and out shall be alike helpful to him: In fellowship with God he shall grow, and in watering others he shall be watered. Having made Jesus his all, he shall find all in Jesus. His soul shall be as a watered garden and as a well of water whose waters fail not.

Yea, I have loved thee with an everlasting love.
JEREMIAH 31:3

$\mathcal{S}$ometimes the Lord Jesus tells His Church His love thoughts. "He does not think it enough behind her back to tell it, but in her very presence He says, 'Thou art all fair, my love.' It is true, this is not His ordinary method; He is a wise lover and knows when to keep back the intimation of love and when to let it out; but there are times when He will make no secret of it; times when He will put it beyond all dispute in the souls of His people" (R. Erskine's Sermons). The Holy Spirit is often pleased, in a most gracious manner, to witness with our spirits of the love of Jesus. He takes of the things of Christ and reveals them unto us. No voice is heard from the clouds, and no vision is seen in the night, but we have a testimony more sure than either of these. If an angel should fly from heaven and inform the saint personally of the Savior's love to him, the evidence would not be one whit more satisfactory than that which is borne in the heart by the Holy Ghost. Ask those of the Lord's people who have lived the nearest to the gates of heaven, and they will tell you that they have had seasons when the love of Christ towards them has been a fact so clear and sure, that they could no more doubt it than they could question their own existence. Yes, beloved believer, you and I have had times of refreshing from the presence of the Lord, and then our faith has mounted to the topmost heights of assurance. We have had confidence to lean our heads upon the bosom of our Lord, and we have no more questioned our Master's affection to us than John did when in that blessed posture; nay, nor so much: For the dark question, "Lord, is it I that shall betray Thee?" has been put far from us. He has kissed us with the kisses of His mouth and killed our doubts by the closeness of His embrace. His love has been sweeter than wine to our souls.

For your sakes he became poor.
2 CORINTHIANS 8:9

The Lord Jesus Christ was eternally rich, glorious, and exalted; but "though he was rich, yet for your sakes he became poor." As the rich saint cannot be true in his communion with his poor brethren unless of his substance he ministers to their necessities, so (the same rule holding with the head as between the members), it is impossible that our Divine Lord could have had fellowship with us unless He had imparted to us of His own abounding wealth and had become poor to make us rich. Had He remained upon His throne of glory, and had we continued in the ruins of the fall without receiving His salvation, communion would have been impossible on both sides. Our position by the fall, apart from the covenant of grace, made it as impossible for fallen man to communicate with God as it is for Belial to be in concord with Christ. In order, therefore, that communion might be compassed, it was necessary that the rich kinsman should bestow His estate upon His poor relatives, that the righteous Saviour should give to His sinning brethren of His own perfection, and that we, the poor and guilty, should receive of His fulness grace for grace; that thus in giving and receiving, the One might descend from the heights, and the other ascend from the depths, and so be able to embrace each other in true and hearty fellowship. Poverty must be enriched by Him in whom are infinite treasures before it can venture to commune; and guilt must lose itself in imputed and imparted righteousness ere the soul can walk in fellowship with purity. Jesus must clothe His people in His own garments, or He cannot admit them into His palace of glory; and He must wash them in His own blood, or else they will be too defiled for the embrace of His fellowship.

O believer, herein is love! For your sake the Lord Jesus "became poor" that He might lift you up into communion with Himself.

Behold, a virgin shall conceive, and bear a son,
and shall call his name Immanuel.
ISAIAH 7:14

Let us today go down to Bethlehem, and in company with wondering shepherds and adoring Magi, let us see Him who was born King of the Jews, for we by faith can claim an interest in Him and can sing, "Unto us a child is born, unto us a son is given." Jesus is Jehovah incarnate, our Lord and our God, and yet our brother and friend; let us adore and admire. Let us notice at the very first glance His miraculous conception. It was a thing unheard of before, and unparalleled since, that a virgin should conceive and bear a Son. The first promise ran thus, "The seed of the woman," not the offspring of the man. Since venturous woman led the way in the sin which brought forth Paradise lost, she, and she alone, ushers in the Regainer of Paradise. Our Savior, although truly man, was as to His human nature the Holy One of God. Let us reverently bow before the holy Child whose innocence restores to manhood its ancient glory; and let us pray that He may be formed in us, the hope of glory. Fail not to note His humble parentage. His mother has been described simply as "a virgin," not a princess or prophetess nor a matron of large estate. True the blood of kings ran in her veins; nor was her mind a weak and untaught one, for she could sing most sweetly a song of praise; but yet how humble her position, how poor the man to whom she stood affianced, and how miserable the accommodation afforded to the newborn King!

Immanuel, God with us in our nature, in our sorrow, in our lifework, in our punishment, in our grave, and now with us, or rather we with Him, in resurrection, ascension, triumph, and Second Advent splendor.

Lo, I am with you alway.
MATTHEW 28:20

The Lord Jesus is in the midst of His church; He walketh among the golden candlesticks; His promise is, "Lo, I am with you alway." He is as surely with us now as He was with the disciples at the lake, when they saw coals of fire and fish laid thereon and bread. Not carnally, but still in real truth, Jesus is with us. And a blessed truth it is, for where Jesus is, love becomes inflamed. Of all the things in the world that can set the heart burning, there is nothing like the presence of Jesus! A glimpse of Him so overcomes us that we are ready to say, "Turn away Thine eyes from me, for they have overcome me." Even the smell of the aloes and the myrrh and the cassia, which drop from His perfumed garments, causes the sick and the faint to grow strong. Let there be but a moment's leaning of the head upon that gracious bosom and a reception of His divine love into our poor cold hearts, and we are cold no longer, but glow like seraphs, equal to every labor, and capable of every suffering. If we know that Jesus is with us, every power will be developed, and every grace will be strengthened, and we shall cast ourselves into the Lord's service with heart and soul and strength; therefore is the presence of Christ to be desired above all things. His presence will be most realized by those who are most like Him. If you desire to see Christ, you must grow in conformity to Him. Bring yourself, by the power of the Spirit, into union with Christ's desires and motives and plans of action, and you are likely to be favored with His company. Remember His presence may be had. His promise is as true as ever. He delights to be with us. If He doth not come, it is because we hinder Him by our indifference. He will reveal Himself to our earnest prayers and graciously suffer Himself to be detained by our entreaties and by our tears, for these are the golden chains which bind Jesus to His people.

Inspirational Library

Beautiful purse/pocket-size editions of Christian classics bound in flexible leatherette. These books make thoughtful gifts for everyone on your list, including yourself!

When I'm on My Knees   The highly popular collection of devotional thoughts on prayer, especially for women.
Flexible Leatherette. $4.97

The Bible Promise Book   Over 1,000 promises from God's Word arranged by topic. What does God promise about matters like: Anger, Illness, Jealousy, Love, Money, Old Age, and Mercy? Find out in this book!
Flexible Leatherette. $3.97

Daily Wisdom for Women   A daily devotional for women seeking biblical wisdom to apply to their lives. Scripture taken from the New American Standard Version of the Bible.
Flexible Leatherette. $4.97

My Daily Prayer Journal   Each page is dated and features a Scripture verse and ample room for you to record your thoughts, prayers, and praises. One page for each day of the year.
Flexible Leatherette. $4.97

Available wherever books are sold.
Or order from:

Barbour Publishing, Inc.
P.O. Box 719
Uhrichsville, OH 44683
http://www.barbourbooks.com

If you order by mail, add $2.00 to your order for shipping.
Prices are subject to change without notice.